Through Their Eyes

Reflections
on
joy, loss,
and
learning

By Nancy Collander

Illustrations by Kevin Collander

Copyright © 2025 Nancy Collander
All rights reserved.
No part of this book may be reproduced, stored in a retrieval system, or transmitted in any form or by any means without the prior express permission of the copyright holder, except for the use of quotations in critical reviews.

Cover and book design: Eric Collander and Rebecca DeNeau
rdeneau.becreative@gmail.com | ecollander.becreative@gmail.com
Cover photo: Eric Collander
Edited by: Kristin D. Zeit, KristinZeit.com

First Edition
Published in the United States of America
by Nancy Collander and Small Farm Publishing
Spring Lake, MI

ISBN 979-8-9988356-0-5 (paperback)
ISBN 979-8-9988356-1-2 (ebook)

This work depicts actual events in the life of the author as accurately as memory permits. All persons (and dogs) are actual individuals. Dialogue is as accurate as my memory allows, except for the dogs', who never let me forget what they said.

*For Sarina and Crystal
at the Morrow County Dog Shelter,
and for the millions of animals in shelters everywhere,
waiting for their chance.*

A portion of all book sales will be donated to the Morrow County
Dog Shelter in Mount Gilead, Ohio.

How is it that with just a look
A nod or a tilt of the head
You can convey, in your own way
What with words could never be said?

How, with the power of speech we have
Can we but only try
To express, without success
What is clear in your soft, dark eye?

Love and loyalty unheard
To rival every spoken word.

Preface

In mid-2016, I was visiting with my sister Beth and we stopped at a local antique mall. My Corgi mix, Spanky, was with me, as usual, and I nestled his little bed into the shopping cart.

"You know, you're becoming one of those crazy old ladies who takes her dog everywhere," Beth observed.

"I know, isn't it great?" I agreed.

This same sister once gave me a kitchen towel imprinted with the slogan: "Dog hair, both a condiment *and* a fashion accessory!" She was never one to mince words, and it was true, anyway. It took me a long time to become this nutty, and many lessons from multiple dogs to be comfortable hearing the truth for what it was, rather than a personal failure.

At the time of Beth's astute observation I was 64. Along life's way, I'd traded my 1970s long, brown hair for a shorter, grayer look, and my skinny, awkward teenage self, had grown into a still-skinny, slightly more self-assured woman. My husband, Kevin, and I had four dogs at this point and had lost eight over the years, so we knew both the joy of being owned by them and the terrible pain when they left us behind. But the thing about dogs is they never stop teaching, and I discovered that their wisdom would come along at exactly the right moment. All I needed to do was look into their eyes. Sometimes I didn't see their full impact until after they passed on; then I understood they were really still with me.

I've always loved animals. My awakening came early, barely out of kindergarten. Walking home from school for lunch one day, I passed snow piled high at the ends of driveways and along the edge of our street. I came around the curve and down the hill; near the curb lay a dead bunny. Curious, I took my mittens off, crying as I picked it up. The fur was so soft, the body so stiff and cold. I remember it as being large, but everything is large when you're a child. Cradling it against my coat, I carried it home, my tears freezing in tiny crystals on the fur. I couldn't leave it there in the road.

Mom opened the door to welcome me in for lunch, and while she must have been horrified to see her daughter lugging home a dead animal, she didn't show it; she saw my unhappy face. Gently, she took the bunny and put it on our enclosed back porch.

"I'm so sorry, honey. I'll bury it later," she soothed me, drying my tears.

With the ground frozen hard as concrete, I'm sure the little body ended up in the trash can. But Mom did the best she could.

Years later as an adult, I retold the story to Mom and she had no recollection of it. It hadn't been a defining moment for her, but it was for me. I remember the sadness deep in my heart, the knowledge of a creature that once was, but now wasn't. It was my first encounter with death. Even now, when I see an animal killed on the road, even a little opossum or chipmunk, I feel the same loss, and there's the knowledge that the world is diminished, just a little, by their ending. The bunny incident was my way of knowing I would never be complete without animals.

My dad and mom began their family in Cleveland, Ohio, in the early 1950s and faced the Herculean task of raising a son and three daughters through the 1960s and '70s. Mom gave up her early-elementary teaching job, transferring all

PREFACE

her love and patience to her children, providing the guidance and foundation we needed to stay on track.

Growing up, my home was stable and happy, but the high expectations my dad set for his children left me with a deep sense of insecurity. Trying to meet someone else's idea of success always eluded me and even though I tried hard in school, my grades were average at best. Evidently, I just wasn't trying hard enough. Somehow, I graduated from high school, but without much sense of self or direction and with a "what's the point?" attitude firmly in place.

Rejecting college, I drifted through my 20s, in and out of jobs and marriage, taking what came my way but not reaching for anything on my own, searching for something but not knowing what. Through all my turmoil, dogs were my anchor—although I didn't realize it then.

I also loved horses and once on my own, I bought my first horse, Missy. My circle of animal-loving friends grew rapidly, and in the late-1970s I met Cindy, the friend who would become my sister-in-law. When personal upheaval required me to sell Missy, Cindy bought her for her son, Eric. I was heartbroken, but at least Missy was in good hands. Shortly thereafter, I met and married Cindy's brother, Kevin, and finally began to find myself.

Kevin and I both grew up with dogs, although neither of us foresaw what a guiding force they'd become. Chance encounters with strays changed the course of our days—and our lives—and cost us money that we often didn't really have to spare. When we adopted, rescued, or took in an otherwise cast-off dog, usually there wasn't much information to go on. But everything we needed to know was right there in their eyes, revealed in one look. We've seen in those looks way too many sad stories. Teaching them to love and trust again was our goal, but we quickly discovered *they* were the teachers, and their lessons were profound.

For those of us who measure the years with dogs, the passage of time flows from one dog to the next—our lives are overlaid with theirs and become inextricable. Events are remembered by the arrival and passage of each dog, and there have been so many that keeping track of who we had when, and whose lives overlapped, became complicated. To keep them all straight, I began my Timeline of Dogs, a spreadsheet of when we got each one, where they came from, each birth date (most were estimates), and the date they passed from our lives. The spreadsheet is the foundation for their stories.

"there is much to be learned from beasts."

— Bram Stoker's *Dracula*

CHAPTER 1
The First, Brief One: 1959

muffin

She was a little mutt, rescued from the shelter to be my very own. I was too young then to understand shelter dogs and missed what her eyes were telling me, the wary look that reflected the insecurity and fear of a life unsettled and uncertain.

As a child, I was transported by stories. Before I learned to read, and way before handheld media or videos, my favorite story was Margaret Wise Brown's *Muffin in the Country*. Mom read it many times and finally (probably to save her sanity), she bought an audio version on a 45 RPM record. In my fort behind the couch, I'd listen to it over and over on my little portable record player. I knew the story by heart but still loved hearing it, and I pictured myself running and playing with the happy little dog. There was no question my first dog would be named Muffin.

When she came into my life on my 7th birthday, I was overjoyed. Muffin was small, with fluffy black and brown hair and folded-over ears, a mix of unknown parentage. This little being was all mine and I spent hours teaching her tricks and rewarding her with treats; she followed me everywhere. My neighborhood friends shared the excitement as we played with her, romping up and down our backyard hill.

I don't remember how long we had her. Of course, her past was a mystery, and I can only assume now she must have been mistreated. One day, in the midst of play with a group of giggling, energetic girls, something frightened Muffin and she bit one of my friends on the cheek. Those were the days before people sued each other at the drop of a hat and, fortunately, the bite wasn't serious. But Dad and Mom couldn't take any chances it might happen again.

I do remember, a few days later, arriving home from school for lunch. In our driveway was a strange truck, and a man in uniform was on the front porch. In his arms was my Muffin. I ran toward him, crying, and ended up in my mother's embrace. As he turned away with my little dog and put

THE FIRST, BRIEF ONE: 1959

her in the truck, I knew she was going away forever. I was heartbroken and never listened to my Muffin record again. I'd learned a hard lesson that things wouldn't always turn out as I wanted.

Years later, Mom shared with me how angry she was at the dog warden; she'd arranged for him to arrive and be gone while I was still at school. I don't know what she would have told me about where Muffin went, but I'm sure it would have been truthful and framed in a way a child could understand. Mom had that way about her.

CHAPTER 2
The Fifth Child: 1960

zipper

His puppy-face was open and innocent, his eyes full of happy expectation, ready for whatever was in store.

After losing Muffin, it wasn't hard to get excited about a new puppy. The biting incident meant my dad chose carefully, settling on an Airedale terrier; a few weeks before Christmas we brought him home. There were other gifts under the tree, but none could match the puppy. I was 8 years old, my brother (David) was 10, and my sister (Susan) was 5. We all welcomed our new playmate and he became our best friend.

As he grew, his energy and playfulness came out, and Zipper became his very-fitting name. Our living room flowed into the kitchen, then into the dining room, and back to the living room in an endless circle, and David, Susan, and I would hide, one around each corner. Zipper chased us until we collapsed in a laughing, dizzy heap.

House training was left mostly up to Mom so I remember little about it, except the patience she showed as he made the connection and learned to woof at the door. While I'm sure there were many indoor accidents, cleaning up the large, fenced backyard soon became part of our to-do list. Taking turns, we learned to use the chore as a bargaining chip when we wanted something from one another.

When Zipper was two years old, my sister Beth was born. I think she was closest to him—he was there the day she came home from the hospital, she grew up with him, and she was still living at home when Zipper died.

As silly kids, we referred to things by known associations so we called Zipper's tail, from the beginning and forever, "the wiener tail." It sure looked like a hot dog to us, and "wiener" was much more fun to say. We delighted in teaching him all kinds of tricks—anything to make his wiener wag—and while he knew the basics, our favorite was to have him sit very still as we placed a treat on his nose. Then, on command, he'd flip the treat in the air and catch it in his mouth. That one astounded all the neighborhood kids, and even earned him a "smartest dog" award at a neighborhood carnival.

But as smart as he was, he could also be pretty bone-headed. If he had something in his mouth he wasn't supposed to, we'd ring the doorbell and he'd race to the door, barking, dropping the forbidden object. The poor dog never figured it out.

Of the four of us, Sue, Beth, and I were the silliest over animals, and some nonsense was always in store. Trying Zipper's infinite patience, we dressed him up in all manner of outfits, from ballerina tutus to Zorro capes, and clipped little red bows into the soft fur above his ears. When Mom came home from the grocery store, we'd help her put away the food, snickering as we swiped the "semi-boneless" sticker from the roast before it went into the freezer. The sticker would find its way onto Zippy's head and we'd laugh until we cried at the sweet, innocent, all-suffering look on his face. He endured much to make his kids happy.

But he also took his role as protector seriously. A small gravel road ran alongside the backyard near our swing set, and if someone walked by while we were playing, Zipper charged the fence, barking and snarling. Our loving, patient companion was also our fierce guardian, a constant presence in our lives, in the yard or on a leash walk. But every so often, he'd sneak out the door into the unfenced front yard and freedom. A neighbor once called to tell Mom her four-legged child was walking up the street—everyone considered Zipper a part of our family.

By the early 1970s, only Sue and Beth were still at home, so David and I weren't close witnesses to Zipper's decline. I remember visiting and noticing how much slower he moved, how he thumped when lying down and struggled to rise. But he was still glad to see me, still wagging his wiener tail; it seemed as though he'd always be there.

Sue was in college, so Beth was on her own the day Zipper left our lives. Dad laid him carefully on several blankets in the back of the station wagon for his last car ride; he asked Beth if she wanted to give Zipper a goodbye pat, but she couldn't bear it. From her bedroom window, she heard the car slowly backing out, turning up the road, and fading away.

After Beth left for college and Dad retired, my parents sold the house and moved to a smaller place. But my memories of the family home and Zipper are intertwined. I drove by the house once, many years later, and pictured him there, sitting on the porch step, waiting for his kids to come home.

While there were cats, both during Zipper's reign and after, he was the one and only family dog. I still have the folder of papers my dad saved when we got Zipper: the litter was born September 25, 1960, and his AKC papers and pedigree, going back five generations, attest to his regal heritage. But to us, he was just Zipper, our best friend, and even without the pedigree we would have loved him the same.

I realize now that back then I thought teaching a dog was a one-way street. Through repetition, he learned to do what I told him, which was enough. I assumed that wisdom was exclusive to people, and so I completely missed the patience

THE FIFTH CHILD: 1960

in his eyes and took for granted the quiet, simple love and loyalty he shared. I now appreciate the things he taught me so long ago.

CHAPTER 3

Our Firstborn: 1984

müsta

A beautiful Black Lab puppy whose eyes spoke of open joy, sharp intelligence, and deep compassion. He charmed us from day one until the end.

Kevin and I always knew dogs would be part of our lives, we had no idea they would *be* our lives. Kevin's huge heart for animals became apparent shortly after we met in 1982, when he stopped by my workplace carrying a coffee can: "Look what I found!" he announced.

Snuggled into a small pile of moss and grass was a tiny mouse, rescued from the road. I knew then that Kevin was the one for me. His love for animals matched mine and there was never any doubt that our life together would always overflow with critters.

Kevin wasn't really a cat person, but my little orange-gold tabby cat was part of the deal and he grew to love her. Wookie was abandoned at birth and I'd hand-raised her, so our bond was strong. As the runt of the litter she was tiny all her life, never weighing more than seven pounds, but her long, fluffy coat made her look bigger. "Star Wars" had been the hot movie when she was born in 1977, and with her round, hairy face and her fearless but gentle demeanor, Wookie was the perfect name.

Kevin and I married in February 1983, and moved to Columbus, Ohio, but our plans to get a dog had to wait. Kevin was home between work assignments in South Africa, and after the wedding the three of us headed off to Johannesburg for a year. In her little crate, Wookie became a world traveler, taking the long trip in stride.

Our new home was near the heart of downtown Johannesburg, a tiny flat on the 15th floor overlooking the city, and before we'd unpacked, Wookie had made a new friend. Two doors away lived Kebra, a beautiful Abyssinian cat that learned our schedule, trotting up to our door each evening for

OUR FIRSTBORN: 1984

playtime with Wookie. After batting a tin-foil ball around for a while, they'd sit side by side at the window, tails twitching, watching the goings-on far below.

The year was filled with ups and downs as we got used to work and life in a foreign country. Our company was there to design dealerships for Volkswagen of South Africa, which meant we had a car at our disposal. But it took a while to understand the maze of Johannesburg's one-way streets, which changed names for no particular reason—it was surely some city planner's idea of a joke. On my first solo excursion, I was nabbed by the local police, pulled over for driving the wrong way on a one-way, buses-only street. The officer peered at my Ohio license, rolled his eyes, then handed me a traffic-laws leaflet and sent me on my way.

Our driving highlight was a work trip to Cape Town—down the N1, through miles of open veldt, then through the mountains near the coast. Design work and sightseeing kept us busy for several weeks, then we packed up and drove to Port Elizabeth before heading back to our Jo'burg flat. Wookie had become our little nomad, traveling along to each temporary home without any fuss, her plastic crate collecting travel stickers as she went.

With our small office staff, the demands of work meant we each wore several hats. But the projects, while stressful, were interesting and fun. Kevin was both designer and project manager, while I filled all the office administration and support roles, from booking flights to running the very old-fashioned Telex machine. It was crazy for a while, but settled somewhat with the addition of three new colleagues, who soon became friends.

Adjusting to marriage was also stressful. Kevin had been a bachelor until we met so we went through our ups and downs, but being so far from home, there was no place to run—we hung together and worked it all out. Overall, it was a wonderful experience which expanded my view of life, and of the world.

It was also the beginning of the winding career path I'd follow until retirement. A Virgo and type-A personality, I'd always been organized, and I possessed an innate curiosity. Growing up, Mom encouraged this: her standard answer to any question was, "Let's go look it up," which meant either the dictionary or *World Book Encyclopedia* in those pre-Internet years. Finding the right answer broadened my knowledge and built my confidence, turning me into a creative, intrepid researcher.

During our time in South Africa, I kept our office running, sourcing construction materials and keeping track of different vendors, and their products and specifications. I became the go-to person, which gave me a sense of accomplishment—maybe I was good at something after all.

At the end of November 1983, with our projects successfully completed, we packed Wookie back in her crate, said goodbye to Kebra, and headed home.

When you're a dog person and you marry a dog person, it's only a matter of time before one moves in and takes over everything. Even before we owned one, our decisions were dog-driven. In January 1984, we put a down payment on a dog-friendly, under-construction condominium in Columbus, and temporarily settled into a flexible-terms apartment near the Ohio State Fairgrounds. The landlord didn't care about much, as evidenced by the marijuana plants on our neighbors' second-floor porch and their very large dog.

Labrador Retrievers are tailor-made for active, outdoor, big-dog people who love the water. A Pisces and former U.S. Coast Guard cadet, Kevin wanted to be in, on, or around the water, and I'd spent childhood summers—all day, nearly every day—at our neighborhood pool. We needed a water dog. The plan was to wait until we were in our condo, but then I discovered a reputable breeder nearby with a new litter of puppies.

"We can just go look, can't we?" I suggested.

"OK, but only to look," Kevin agreed.

Neither of us was under any illusions. I surreptitiously tucked the checkbook into my purse.

From the unbearably cute mound of three-day-old puppies we reserved the largest black male, and several weeks later he let us know we were his, trotting over and melting us with huge puppy eyes. It was hard to wait until he was old enough to bring home. An English Lab, he was square and compact in the body with a broad head and, even for a pup, large paws. His mother, Babo, was a sweet-natured Black, with a bold, independent streak—the breeder said she left her pups each day to go for her pond swim. The dad, Justin Case, was a sensible, outgoing Yellow.

Now, what to name our new boy? Something unique, of course, since he would be the most special Black Lab in all the world. Starting with Kevin's Finnish heritage, we began looking at translations and came up with Müsta Koira, which means "black dog."[1] "Müsta" had a big, bold sound; it was easy to say and was certainly unique. He was the breeder's first-ever puppy with a Finnish name.

Wookie hadn't been consulted, but after all she'd been through in her life with me, I knew the impending chaos wouldn't faze her. Fulfilling my dad's worst fears, my wandering 20s had seen two failed marriages, several other relationships, four or five low-paying jobs, and multiple moves. Wookie had followed along as if upheaval was the norm. All that, plus the jaunt to South Africa and back, made her the most unflappable cat ever—a puppy would be no sweat.

True to his breed, Müsta was a swimmer and fetcher from the day we brought him home, and his large water bowl was constantly half-empty since he splashed around in it and stuck his face in the water. I'd put a set of Juggling for Dummies bean-bag cubes in Kevin's stocking the previous Christmas and, since both of us were dummies, they became Müsta's first fetching toys. They were the perfect size for his little mouth and he loved the way they skittered across the hardwood floor. He'd proudly trot back to us, gently holding the prize.

Wookie established the ground rules on day one, controlling Müsta's puppy exuberance with not-so-subtle intimidation; a few swats on Müsta's nose put him firmly in his place as second banana. But Wookie loved to play, too, frequently joining in the fetch, batting the bean bags around and keeping up with her new brother (the bean bags lasted until Müsta started teething).

---

[1]. The Finnish language has no ü (u-umlaut) but we thought it looked cool, so we created one. We pronounced Müsta's name MOO-stah.

OUR FIRSTBORN: 1984

Another joint activity was roach hunting. College students and other tenants constantly moving in and out of an old apartment building was an open invitation to cockroaches and, try as we might, there was no way to get rid of them completely. Wookie and Müsta chased them around the baseboards, jumped up the walls, and crawled under the furniture; it was cheap entertainment. We anticipated leaving the roaches behind with the fall completion of our condo.

Müsta quickly outgrew his water-bowl pool, and a plastic kiddie pool appeared on the apartment's front porch. Dunking his Tennis the Menace ball became Müsta's favorite game as he pawed it under the water, then barked and pounced when it popped back up. Always into things, he spied an empty plastic gallon-sized milk jug in the recycling bucket, and soon enough it found its way into the pool, bobbing around with the tennis balls. Grabbing the jug by the handle, he looked like a big black ant carrying a giant breadcrumb. Everything was an adventure.

As the center of our universe, Müsta received constant attention, so training was easy. The nearby fairgrounds gave him plenty of room to run, and lessons overlapped with fetch playtime as he learned to "drop it," "sit," and "release." For socialization, we enrolled him in a group class and he was sure we'd arranged the big party especially for him—he wasn't a star pupil, but he learned how to interact with other dogs and earned his diploma.

I admit we were not the most demanding parents when it came to obedience, and Müsta figured that out very early, using his monkeyshines behavior to con us into occasionally bending the rules. Reading us perfectly, he tested how much he could get away with until he had us pegged, and we knew he was doing it. But he also understood what he couldn't get away with; we balanced the discipline and he thrived.

Müsta was such a people magnet! Sunny Sunday afternoons found us lounging on the Oval at The Ohio State University, where my sister Beth was a student, and the kids passing by made a big fuss over him, tossing his toys and giving him all the attention he so rightly deserved. It was there he learned to follow us and come when we called. True to his independent streak, "come" was hard for him, but if he refused to follow, we walked away.

"Bye, Müsta. Mom and Dad are going."

Watching to see if we were really leaving him behind, he wouldn't let us get far before he'd come tearing after us. Throughout his life, he never lagged behind while hiking off-leash or rambled more than 100 yards or so ahead without turning back, demanding to know if we were coming.

Müsta went with us nearly everywhere and as his world expanded he became a confident, fearless explorer. One freedom of apartment living was time to spend however we wanted: no grass mowing, snow shoveling, or maintenance. Weekends were our own and Müsta developed a keen sense of the passing days, always knowing when Saturday arrived. The only decision we had was which park to visit and how much stuff to take, a day's worth of supplies or just enough for the morning.

Alum Creek State Park was a favorite destination and we spent late summer weekends hiking and swimming. A rented canoe introduced Müsta to boating and, not knowing what his reaction would be, we kept his leash on. Good thing we did.

OUR FIRSTBORN: 1984

Müsta was enthralled. He'd been in the water many times, but never *on* it, so he did the natural thing and jumped overboard, bobbing under briefly before popping up, surprised but not afraid. Our next purchase was a puppy life vest.

On Halloween weekend 1984, we packed up everything but the cockroaches and moved into our condominium. Between work, travel, and puppyhood, our first two years of marriage had been hectic, and we all looked forward to settling down and building a sense of permanence in a home of our own. But life had other plans for us.

I suppose there are people who can pick up and go without a thought, whose lives and time are all their own. There might have even been such a month or two in my own distant past. But "What about the critters?" drove all of our decisions, and in February 1985, as Müsta's first birthday approached, an opportunity arose that required a tough choice.

It was another overseas work project, this time in Australia. Quarantine laws required putting Müsta and Wookie in a government-run kennel for six months once we arrived, which we weren't willing to do. But we agonized over leaving our kids behind—if we couldn't find the perfect solution for their care, we wouldn't make the trip.

Beth volunteered to take Wookie, and Carl, a good family friend who'd recently lost his old Lab, was more than willing to take Müsta. Carl lived alone near a lake, so our boy would have lots of attention and swimming. As hard as it was, we said goodbye to Müsta and Wookie for 10 months.

Our flat in Kirribilli was directly across the harbor from the Sydney Opera House, and there was water everywhere! Without a car on this trip, we walked a lot, pretending Müsta was with us—how he would have loved all the parks and beaches, the walk up and over the Harbour Bridge, and the ferry rides. We missed him terribly, but Carl's letters and pictures said they were having fun and, aside from chewing up a pair of Florsheim shoes, Müsta was being a good boy.

But we should have known better than to think we could remain critterless for long. Even with all the new things to do and places to explore, life in our little flat felt empty, so we made a trip to the Sydney RSPCA and Kissa—"cat" in Finnish—came into our lives. Huddled on a carpet-covered perch near the ceiling of the shelter, she looked so forlorn; she'd been at the shelter most of her young life.

"We'll take her," we said in unison.

A sweet caramel-and-white tabby with beautiful yellow eyes, Kissa immediately took to Kevin (the non-cat person), curling up on the small of his back as he dozed on the floor in front of the TV. Each day, we took the ferry home from work and there she'd be in the window, watching and waiting, happy to have a place to belong.

Our apartment building was only four floors but had an elevator, and what we assumed was a stray cat who hung out in the car park on the ground floor. Shortly after we moved in, we discovered he actually lived on the top floor, two above us; he'd often wait by the elevator for a ride up. Once inside, we'd push the button for him and when we exited, the Elevator Cat continued his ride home. Some mornings when

OUR FIRSTBORN: 1984

we left for work, there he was on his daily ride down, off to do whatever cats do on the Sydney waterfront.

The work projects on this trip included store design for Just Jeans (Australia's answer to The Gap), and a small chain of handbag shops. Two of our U.S. office colleagues had traveled with us, so the workload, while stressful, was more balanced. Two locals also joined our team, easing us into work and play in Sydney and giving us the inside scoop on places to see and things to do. As it happened, a few weeks after we arrived, the QE2 luxury ocean liner came into port, the Concorde flew in from London, and they exchanged their well-heeled passengers. Arising early, nearly the entire population of Sydney turned out to greet the ship, lining the waterfront and crowding the Harbour Bridge, cheering, waving, and (of course) drinking. Not much work was done that Thursday as our entire office staff joined the festivities and, while Australians don't need much of an excuse for a party, the event was huge by anyone's standards.

A water lover's paradise, Sydney had ferries that ran all day every day to the multitude of beaches, and we took full advantage. While it was chilly—our internal calendars said it was summer, but the southern hemisphere said otherwise—and our flat had no central heat, sunny weekend days found us at the beach or dining and dancing on the outdoor Forecourt of the Sydney Opera House, soaking up the atmosphere. But the longer we were away from Müsta and Wookie, the more we missed them, and as our projects wound down, we were ready for home.

Right before Thanksgiving 1985, we headed back to the USA, detouring for a six-day vacation in Fiji. Once back in Columbus we tossed our luggage in the condo and went straight to Carl's. Müsta was taller and had filled out to nearly his adult weight, but he'd retained his puppy silliness, rolling on his back and cavorting with excitement. We were all so happy to see each other! After a long walk around the lake, we collected Müsta's belongings as he leaned against our car door. *You are not leaving me this time!* his eyes clearly conveyed. It was hard for Carl to see him go and shortly thereafter, he got another Lab of his own.

After picking up Wookie we settled back together again, and our misgivings about leaving them for so long proved unfounded. They were so easygoing, and we all picked up where we left off.

Kissa arrived a few days later, right on schedule. Who knew there was a company dedicated to shipping pets around the world? They took care of the crating, food, water, paperwork, and vaccination regulations, and kept track of her during the trip. After initial rounds of hissing and general wariness, our two globe-trotting felines got along well. But Müsta loved Kissa right away; this began our awareness of his compassionate soul. He understood that she felt unsettled at first and treated her gently. She responded by becoming his best buddy. The three shared sunny sleeping spots by the windows and winter nights in front of the fireplace, curled together in Müsta's bed. The condo was our home for the next nine years.

Looking back on 1985, it's hard to believe we left Müsta and Wookie at all, and that at one point we actually considered staying in Australia. Thinking now about all the dogs of our lives, we're so glad our critters drew us back home.

OUR FIRSTBORN: 1984

Opportunity knocks in strange ways sometimes. After being away from home and pets, the last thing we wanted was more upheaval. But in 1986, the company we worked for was purchased by, and absorbed into, a larger, internationally respected design firm. Although I didn't realize it at the time, it would have a positive effect on me personally and was the most important and influential event in my professional life. Tasked with building about 300 or so boxes of the firm's design books and materials into a working library, I thought, how hard could it be? I'm great at organizing!

I tackled the project head-on; it was more difficult than I anticipated but I'd never been one to back down from a challenge. Enrolling in the company's tuition-assistance program, I finally went to college to pursue a degree in library and information science at Ohio Dominican University. Balancing school and work, after six years I graduated summa cum laude.

Earning that degree was my first big success. Still lurking in the back of my mind was my ingrained sense of failure, of not being able to live up to my dad's expectations. In the early 1970s, I'd earned an associate's degree in equine management but never did anything with it. Dad had paid the tuition, so I'd disappointed him again. But this degree was something I'd done on my own. I'd set a goal, tried my hardest, and succeeded, and in my secret heart I felt vindicated, since Dad and Mom witnessed this achievement. I also discovered I was actually good at something I liked.

Drawing on my love of research, I began offering the design teams information to support their projects, which was fascinating for me and broadened my knowledge. The company specialized in industrial, graphic, and retail design, opening up a wide variety of research opportunities. Honing my skills, I became adept at rooting out quality information from reliable sources and packaging it in formats useful to the teams. From a jumble of boxes to an organized library, I was now in charge of a valuable information resource. I thrived with the company for 17 years.

Among my new colleagues was a large group of animal lovers and many became lifelong friends. We built a network of rescue connections, helped one another with animals in need, and sometimes brought sick or injured pets into the office. The company encouraged our efforts, and the library provided a quiet refuge for various critters, recuperating as their owners worked. Any given day might find a crate or two tucked back in the corner of the library, or an elderly dog curled up under my desk.

Not caring for the large-company environment, Kevin left the firm in late 1987, and joined some former colleagues in a smaller setting. The design industry in Columbus at the time was thriving and incestuous, with designers company-hopping based on opportunity and who had the coolest projects, never burning bridges and always remaining friends. Kevin is also a watercolorist, and he found success in the large Columbus arts community. Blending his degree in architecture and love of design, he was inspired by the city's historic buildings, and cityscape paintings became his signature. The portable easel often came along on our outdoor adventures and while Müsta and I played, Kevin created.

OUR FIRSTBORN: 1984

Müsta was such a joy! He had his momma Babo's bold streak and his daddy Justin's gentle aura, combined into his own curious, inventive nature and creative playfulness—and he was very smart. From the beginning, our critters were our children and we talked to them constantly. But while the cats pretty much ignored us, Müsta listened intently, building a vocabulary of favorite words and conveying his feelings through his eyes.

Like most Labs, his puppy energy remained for many years, and along with his outdoor play, indoor outlets were a must. A large bucket overflowed with all manner of stuffed toys, balls, and rope pulls, and it was always tipped over.

"Hey, I just picked these up! Who spread all these toys around again?" I'd ask with a sly smile, hands on hips.

Not me, Mom. Must have been the cats! He tried to act innocent, but it never worked.

My sewing machine was always busy, stitching up torn stuffed animals and making catnip mice and dog beds. There was at least one bed on each floor of the house. The big, black fleece one in the living room was Müsta's favorite—such a favorite he'd grab it by a corner, gather the bed underneath himself, and, even though he was neutered, hump it in circles all around the room. Since married people have to get serious about things like insurance, one evening Kevin and I sat with an agent at the dining room table, trying our best to keep straight faces while behind him, Müsta was going at it with the bed, bumping into the walls and furniture. Why the agent didn't hear the commotion and turn around, and how we maintained our self-control, I will never know!

But serious Müsta-play required his Tennis the Menace ball, and to avoid throwing it indoors we invented Knock-over, a raucous, action-packed game full of barking, yelling, and lots of rolling around on the floor. Holding the ball to his chest, Kevin would lie on his stomach while Müsta proceeded to nudge, lick, and push Kevin's shoulders and neck, trying to roll him over to pounce on the ball. It was great fun, but it didn't take Müsta long to get bored and figure out a new twist: diving in with his nose aimed at Kevin's crotch, Kevin shouted and immediately rolled over, exposing the ball.

Another favorite was soccer. A hallway in our finished lower level connected to Kevin's art studio and, dropping his tennis ball in the studio doorway, Müsta would bark, requiring Kevin to get up and play. Kicking the ball past Müsta down the hall scored a goal, and Müsta became adept at watching the angle of Kevin's foot, anticipating which direction the ball would go. Kevin didn't win very often. Errant kicks often hit the walls on either side of the doorway, leaving gross, slobbery splats, while happy barks and shouts of "Goal!" and "Hey, no cheating!" floated up to me from below.

Still, outdoor activity was Müsta's preference and weekday evenings he was wound up, ready for fun.

"Want to go swimming at Antrim Park?" Silly question! The nearby park became a regular destination, with a hike around the lake and then an hour or two of swim-fetch. Not content to simply run into the lake, Müsta would charge the water, leaping high to make a huge splash, and fetch the ball no matter how far we threw it.

"OK, one more throw!" He'd stay all night if we let him. Ever the creative, independent boy, he'd employ stall tactics when it was time to head home, retrieving the ball but then loitering on his way back, sniffing things and getting purposely distracted. To prolong the play, we often walked him over to the park's tennis courts.

"Go find 'em!"

Instantly in hunt mode, Müsta would race back and forth, searching for tennis balls in the woods behind the courts. Some he found were nearly new, others brown and moss-covered, and he once brought one that had been in the woods for ages—it was cracked, the skin was nearly gone, and a small tree sprouted from inside. But, what the heck, it was a tennis ball, so he fetched it.

After our time in Sydney, the sailing bug bit Kevin and we bought a 14 foot sailboat and trailer, spending our weekends on the lake at Alum Creek State Park. Having done his Coast Guard 4th Class summer cruise aboard the *Eagle*, Kevin was a natural sailor, and our little boat was so easy I soon earned my role as first mate. Müsta would catch the scent of the lake long before we'd arrive at the dock and remain on alert until the boat was in the water with the sail up. Assuming his role as commander, Müsta supervised his crew and when we finally pulled up the centerboard and beached in a sandy cove, he'd wait for the "OK!" before we all jumped in for a cool-off swim. At a year and a half old, he was the light of our lives and the center of all our activities.

We literally cruised through the summer of 1986, sailing nearly every weekend. One mid-summer afternoon, across the lake, a mile or two away, dark clouds gathered over the tree line, headed our way. The sailing had been great with a light, consistent breeze and as we tacked back and forth across the lake, Müsta snuggled on his foam pad in the low spot below the boom, his head resting on the side rails.

But the clouds were moving in fast so we headed for the dock, as did all the other boaters. We almost made it. The sky grew darker and the wind became erratic; we caught what there was, but about 200 feet from shore it went dead calm. Müsta sat up, sensing danger. A few minutes later the wild wind and rain swept in and our little boat was caught in the whirling storm. Over she went, dumping us all into the lake. Our life vests brought us up safely, but the water was so shallow the mast stuck in the muddy lake bottom, and Kevin decided to stay with the boat.

"Go! Swim for it!" he yelled over the wind.

As I treaded water, Müsta kept circling me, the concern clear in his eyes. Then I gripped the back of his vest and he struck out strongly, heading straight for the shore to save his mom. In the meantime, several boaters came to Kevin's rescue, freed and righted the sailboat, and towed it to the dock. Huddling under the picnic shelter, I held Müsta back so he didn't charge off to save Kevin, as well.

"It's OK, buddy," I reassured him. "Dad's fine."

But he whined and barked, watching intently as Kevin tied up the boat and ran toward us to wait out the storm. After we were all safely together, Müsta finally relaxed. It made me realize how loyal and protective he was. Just as he was our whole world, we were his. I began to see the world through his eyes.

The boat also went along on camping weekends and as we pulled out the gear and began packing, Müsta was ready; his food, tennis ball, and first aid kit were all he needed. If

OUR FIRSTBORN: 1984

only we could travel that light! Our circle of friends included many campers, and all manner of accommodations, from pup tents to trailers, converged as we crammed in as many weekend getaways as possible. The large group meant lots of playtime for Mü, running and fetching as long as someone threw the ball. As the evenings mellowed and the conversation lagged, he'd crash around the campfire, but he soon learned the tent was much safer. A black dog in the darkness was easily stepped on. Standing nose to the tent flap, he'd woof to be let in and when we crawled in later, there he'd be, stretched full-length across the sleeping bags, 85 pounds of snoring Lab for us to curl around.

When winter stepped in, interrupting the sailing and camping, weekend days meant long, snowy walks in the woods at Alum Creek. One hike at the end of winter 1993 brought an unexpected gift into our lives.

CHAPTER 4

A Life, Saved: 1993

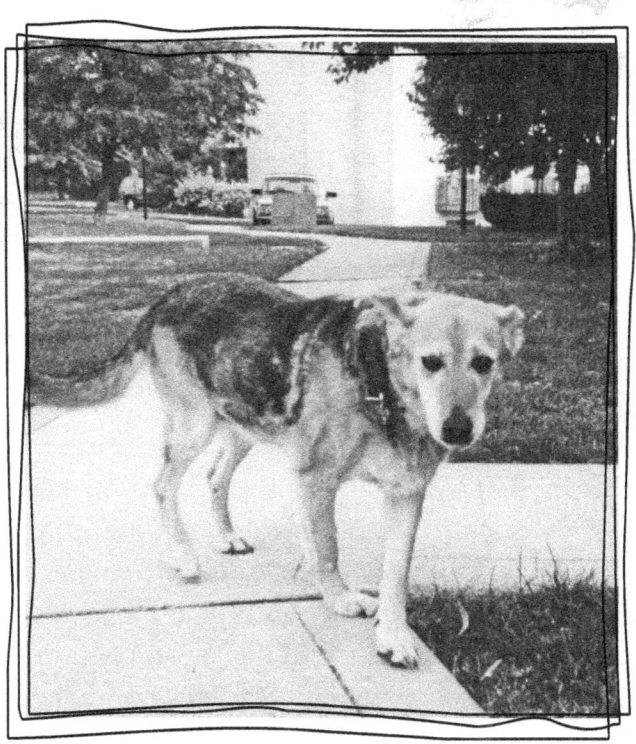

Lapsi

Defeat. All hope was gone and in her eyes was only blankness; nothing. We'll never know how she came to be where we found her, or why the paths of our lives crossed at all. She laid about 10 feet off the trail in the winter grass, and we would have walked right past her if not for Müsta.

In late March 1993, we headed out early for a walk in the woods, stopping on the way for breakfast at our favorite diner. As we ate, a cold misty rain began that promised to continue all day, and we nearly canceled our hike. But Müsta expected the outing and was waiting patiently in the truck.

Having argued about something at breakfast (money, I think), our moods were as sullen as the weather as we set off into the woods. The mist hung like damp curtains in the chilly trees, and from high above, large drops of water fell from the remaining leaves, hitting the layers of forest floor with loud plops. Beyond the trees the lake was silent and dark, little whitecaps whipped up in the breeze. All the power boats, WaveRunners, and swimmers had disappeared; for now, it was quiet and peaceful.

Kevin and I walked silently side by side, each of us lost in thought as Mü ranged ahead, sweeping wide arcs across the path, checking out each tree, and sniffing under every log and leaf pile. Once in a while, he'd scare up a bunny and give chase, but only for fun. When a downed branch caught his fancy he'd carry it until something more interesting came along. Sometimes we'd toss his stick into the woods and after a short search and much crashing around, he'd return, tail wagging, with the very same branch, plucked from a million others exactly like it.

But no matter how many sticks or distractions he found, his real goal was the lake. On we hiked toward the water, watching him enjoy himself, when suddenly he froze, nose in the air, and took off in a straight line after a scent only he could detect, his frantic tail indicating a serious find. He stopped, sniffing intently at something in the grass, and

A LIFE, SAVED: 1993

turned to us with a familiar urgency in his eyes: *Dad, Mom, you'd better come look!*

We approached and were met with a sorry sight. In a tight ball, surrounded by a nest of damp grass, lay an old dog. She looked up, barely raising her head, and her tail wagged weakly against the wet ground. If not for her eyes, she could have been part of the landscape—so dirty and brown was her coat, as soggy and miserable as the dead leaves underfoot.

"Good boy, Müsta!" He sat proudly nearby and oversaw the rescue.

Whatever we were arguing about earlier vanished in our concern for the poor dog. Kneeling beside her, we saw the white in her muzzle and the silver tufts above her eyes, but otherwise it was impossible even to guess her color. Gently, we checked her over for wounds, helped her up and the horror of her condition became obvious. Matted with burrs, she stood stiffly, wavering slightly. Ribs showed plainly through her filthy, pathetic coat, her body thinned to nearly nothing at the waist, and the knobs of her spine stood out like the knuckles of a man's hand. As if ashamed of her condition, she lowered her head and began to shiver. She was wet nearly to the skin.

Lab owners know to carry towels, so we pulled several from our backpack and wrapped up the old dog. Treats were another thing we carried and after rewarding Müsta for his find, we fed the rest to the towel-wrapped skeleton; she was obviously hungry but ate slowly and drank only a little water. Needing a break from our chilly hike we sat, huddled close together on a damp log, rubbing the old dog to warm her. Our Thermos held enough coffee for a cup each and we savored it, the cups warming our fingers.

There was no question we'd take her with us; we needed to get her warm and dry, but she could barely stand and certainly couldn't walk. As I strapped on the backpack, Kevin snugged the towels around the old girl and bundled her into his arms.

The hike out was long and we stopped several times to rest. She was a large dog and quite an armload even in her emaciated state. Ignoring sticks, sniffs, and bunnies, Müsta paced himself to our slow progress, looking up frequently with worry in his eyes. Back at the truck, we laid her on the floor by the heat vent and headed to our veterinarian.

Müsta was a favorite at the clinic and as we recounted the rescue, he wagged and wiggled under the petting and praise of the staff. In the exam room, we set the old girl on the scale, removed the towels, and the staff gasped: she weighed only 34 pounds. By now she was warm and smelled terrible, but Dr. Miley knelt beside her and began the gentle examination. He guessed her to be between 12 and 14 years old, a German Shepherd/Collie cross mixed with who knows what else. In her mouth were brown stubs where most of her teeth should have been, cataracts clouded her eyes, and she barely responded when the vet clapped, so her hearing was also mostly gone. After finding no wounds or injuries, Dr. Miley gave her the basic injections and we decided against a heartworm test; if she was positive she'd never survive the treatment. Her immediate needs were food, water, and a bath, so we packed everybody back in the truck and headed home.

In the basement near the furnace, we made her a comfy bed out of the bottom half of a large plastic dog crate. But before sleep, she had a bath. Several, in fact.

"C'mon, kid, let's get you cleaned up," Kevin said, lifting her easily into the laundry tub.

She was too weak to resist as he lathered, rinsed, and repeated until the tub was full of hair clumps and dirt and the drain was hopelessly clogged. I toweled her dry, filling the air with soft, creamy fluff from her undercoat. As I smiled into the sweet, damp face between my toweled hands, her eyes showed a gratitude and relief that went to my heart.

"You're safe now, sweet girl," I said. "We love you." Being warm and clean must have felt so good.

The black saddle pattern, tan legs, and feathery tail hair showed her German Shepherd side, but her face had the Collie point. Her ears did a funny flop halfway up, as if they couldn't decide whether to stand up straight or hang down, and each had its own odd angle, making her head look cocked to one side. She was a mystery mutt, but we didn't really care what she was, as long as she wasn't dying out in the woods, all alone.

After a little food and water she fell asleep instantly, and the first few days she slept so deeply we had to shake her awake to eat and go outside. Several times I was sure she'd died, her breathing was so shallow and she was so hard to wake up. But each time, she got up, wagging her tail and ready for whatever was next.

Once clean, her coat was quite pretty. I groomed her gently, a little each day, since there was nothing between the hair and the bones beneath but a layer of tender skin; no nice padding of fat to cushion the brush. She had hair knots everywhere, embedded deeply, and I worked at each one with my fingers to pick them loose and pull them out.

Usually, Müsta sat with me and supervised the care of his foundling. He was very gentle with her, as he was with anyone or anything he perceived to be weaker or more fragile, and as I watched him with her I began to fully realize the depth of his compassion. If she fell asleep without finishing her food, he'd look at me, not asking if he could have it but worried she hadn't eaten. When we woke her to go outside before bedtime Müsta went along, walking close to her in the dark and guiding her back inside to bed. Once she was asleep and we closed the door on the snoring old girl, Müsta finally relaxed his watch.

Kevin had been calling her "kid," but she needed a real name. In the Finnish dictionary, we found "child," so we named her Lapsi. Whether she understood her new name we never knew, but with or without a name she was happy; she belonged to someone again.

Walking tentatively, Lapsi could only handle a turn with Müsta around the backyard at first. Our neighbor always came out to pet them both and remark on the progress Lapsi was making, but in truth she was barely holding on. She needed several small meals each day until she was stable, so off she'd go to work with me, her crate-bed tucked behind my desk. Lapsi became a favorite at the office, and as visitors knelt and fussed over her, she thumped her tail softly, raising her head at the touch of each hand, drawing strength from the love.

As she grew stronger and more mobile, Lapsi moved out of the laundry room and became an official member of the family. Our condo association rules allowed only one dog, but our dog-loving neighbor was the association president and we discovered it paid to have friends in high places. A silent shadow, Lapsi would follow us—me in particular—and wherever I was, Lapsi was, too. True to her Shepherd heritage, she herded me constantly and never laid down if I was standing or moving around. If I was behind a closed door she'd stand with her nose to the jamb until I reappeared. She'd been lost once, and she didn't intend to be lost again.

Lapsi ignored Wookie and Kissa, and was housebroken, so it stood to reason she was once someone's pet. On her initial vet visit, Dr. Miley felt what he believed to be a spay scar on her tummy, so someone had cared for her at some point. This bothered me so much. The woods where we found her were nowhere near any housing, and she was in such poor shape she couldn't have walked that far. Although I knew people could be cruel and heartless, it didn't seem possible to me that someone who once loved her just tossed her away. I couldn't picture someone carrying her to the middle of the woods and setting her down, leaving her to wander around, half blind, searching for her person. Maybe she'd gone off by herself to die alone, the way animals will do, and walked until she couldn't go any further. I'd never know, but it haunted me anyway.

Before Lapsi, Müsta had been our only child and we worried he might be jealous. But Lapsi was his foundling and he understood she was no threat. He cared for her as he'd done with Kissa.

Even as a young dog, Müsta expressed compassion for both people and other animals; once, at Antrim Park Lake, he sniffed along the shore and then stopped suddenly, wagging frantically, an urgent concern in his eyes. He'd found a robin, tangled in fishing line and nearly ready to drop into the water. Müsta watched as Kevin carefully cut and unwound the line, then set the exhausted bird in the crook of a nearby tree to recover. It was the first of Müsta's rescues and we soon learned to recognize his look: *You'd better come see.* Over the years, he guarded the neighbor's children from the road, worried over stray cats, and comforted our foster animals. But rescuing Lapsi was his proudest moment. He was 10 years old when he found her, his place secure in our home and hearts, and he was more than willing to share us.

About four weeks after we brought Lapsi home, she had the first in a series of small strokes and reverted almost to the way we found her. She stopped eating, slept nearly all the time, and lost most of the weight she'd gained. Each day was borrowed time but we wanted so much for her to survive, and she must have wanted it too, because she fought her way back again and again. Finally, she was firmly on the road to recovery and as we headed into the coming fall and winter, we were sure she'd be with us for some time.

As her health returned, she continued to gain weight and energy, her coat became shiny and soft, and the helplessness vanished from her eyes. During her first several months with us she hadn't made a sound, and when she finally barked it surprised her as much as it did us. She seemed unfamiliar with her own voice—a high, yippy sound, strange for a large dog. But most of the time she was quiet, even when Müsta alerted us to someone at the door.

Lapsi also began to show a real personality and turned out to be quite a character. Wherever she went, she never walked; instead, she trotted like Edith Bunker from "All in the Family," hurrying from room to room as though every task were urgent. And her tail kept us in stitches. Even though life had treated her badly her tail was always wagging—and she *really* wagged it! It moved at its own odd rhythm and only stopped when she fell asleep, as though she'd worn herself out wagging her tail.

Kevin's mother passed away not long before we found Lapsi, and since his mom had loved polka music, we played it once in a while. One evening, the music was lively and Müsta was rolling around with one of his many toys while Lapsi stood between us.

"Watch her tail!" Kevin laughed.

It was wagging in time with the music. With each new tune, it switched up the tempo, swinging perfectly to the beat. I nearly fell on the floor laughing. The innocent happiness in her eyes, and the joy she brought us, earned her a loving hug. It was a moment we never forgot.

Winter arrived and while Müsta loved all weather, snow was his favorite. But as much as he loved it, Lapsi hated it. Our fussy little old lady didn't want to get her feet wet and if the sidewalks hadn't been shoveled, she'd pick her way along in the footprints of others, stopping when she got too cold. In the rain she stayed glued to our legs under the umbrella and wouldn't relieve herself until we stepped away. There we'd stand, in the rain, holding the umbrella out over her—our next step in becoming crazy dog people.

Fall 1994 brought our first monumental change, spurred by a family heartbreak. The year before, my sister Sue had been diagnosed with very aggressive cancer—the odds were not good, even with treatment. Three years apart in age, we were very close and always there for each other. I admired her greatly and stood with her as she battled on her own terms, with her unique sense of style, humor, and determination. Sue passed away in May '94, gracefully accepting the inevitable, and as I staggered through the summer in a fog of grief, the passage of time weighed on me. Living in the country always appealed to us, especially for Müsta, and I would turn 42 in the fall. What were we waiting for?

The Realtor and I went to see a mini-farm one day while Kevin was working, and from the first moment, I felt we were destined to live there. I had an immediate, deep connection to the place and was instantly at home. We bought the property and moved from the condo.

Located in Morrow County, about 40 miles northeast of Columbus, the property had originally been part of a 100-acre farm owned by a man named Frank Turner. After his estate sale, the land was divided, we bought the house and 7.5 acres, and my brother-in-law bought the adjacent 7 acres as an investment. In the middle of our field, an oil well chugged day and night like a far-off train. The oil rights didn't transfer, so each day a truck from the well-maintenance company drove down our driveway to reach the well path, which we dubbed Turner Trail. Müsta and Lapsi looked forward to the visits, since the driver loved dogs and always handed out treats.

Our house was very old, built of hand-hewn timbers between 1842 and 1847, and sat at a crossroads that had once been the little town of Penlan. The property's barn was a converted one-room schoolhouse, complete with sections of chalkboard and a bell tower (minus the bell, unfortunately). Across the two-lane road to the west sat the tiny Mt. Pisgah Primitive Baptist Church, which held services just once a month, and beyond it were 250 acres of farmland. We were surrounded by working farms. Along the back of our property and down through a neighbor's woods ran the south branch of the Kokosing River, but we called it Owl Creek for the hooting back in the woods. The history of our little corner was captivating.

We met the new neighbors, began working on the house, and eased into the quiet of rural living.

Had we really thought about it, we might have stayed in Columbus. Culture shock set in as we traded carefree condo living for outdoor chores and house renovations. Although livable, the house was a true fixer-upper. We'd spend the next 27 years working on MüFarm.

Animal people always find one another, usually without really trying, and we quickly started collecting new friends. Missy, the horse I'd owned years before and had sold to Kevin's sister Cindy, returned to me, but until our barn was ready I needed a place for her. Through our Realtor, Becky Payne, we met Mike and Susie Baird, two houses south; they had a stall available.

Technically, Missy still belonged to Cindy. But she lived in the city and her son no longer rode, so we shared ownership—I always told people I married Kevin to get my horse back! As one of many MüFarm projects, adding a stall to our barn took a while, but eventually the mission was accomplished and Missy came home, back with me after 20 years.

The Bairds became more like family than friends. Susie and I traded horse- and dog-sitting as needed, treating each other's animals as our own, and her Golden Retriever, CiCi, became an extension of our pack. Sneaking over to MüFarm to play, CiCi would make herself at home, ransacking the toy bucket and picking out her toy du jour. More than once, the Bairds called us to check on their wayward child and CiCi would stay and play with her "cousins" until Susie picked her up. Mike became our remodeling contractor, arriving each morning as we were leaving for work, and the dogs loved him.

Remodeling an old house presented challenges at every turn and we learned to anticipate the roadblocks. Our first interior project required Mike to re-route the upstairs bathroom plumbing to accommodate a huge support beam, and from that point on the domino effect ruled. Even the simplest-looking projects required at least two or three additional steps, taking much longer than planned and costing a lot more. Oh, well; we were (relatively) young, energetic, and game for any challenge.

Lapsi was upset by the move at first, but soon realized she wouldn't be abandoned again and settled in. Wookie and Kissa loved the house right away; the field mice that had taken up residence in the basement kept them both occupied. Müsta was in heaven! The property had been vacant over the summer, and bunnies and mice ran wild in the overgrown fields and hedgerows. He chased them constantly, rooting them from their nests and holes, but he always allowed his prey to escape.

Exploring the surrounding area, Missy, Müsta, and I followed the rural roads and wandered the woodland trails through what we called Penlan Park—acres of woods belonging to a friendly neighbor. Sometimes Kevin hiked along while Müsta ranged ahead, crisscrossing the paths and checking out Owl Creek, a Lab in all his wet, happy glory.

Fall lasted well into November, with sunny days and a touch of evening chill. Weekends saw visits from family and friends, and we spent hours outside, walking the fields and becoming part of the farm. Lapsi followed closely as she did inside the house, but if she strayed or lagged behind, Müsta was there to guide her back; she was strong enough to go a good distance if we paced ourselves. Week nights, after work and chores we'd relax in the yard, sipping wine and playing Tennis the Menace endlessly. One of these evenings became my most vivid and cherished memory of Lapsi.

Several beautiful old maple trees towered over the front of our house, flamed gold and red by the recent nights' chill. The sunlight, slanting across the yard, highlighted each leaf in its own glory, giving everything the special glow that appears only near sunset in late fall. While Kevin threw the ball for Mü, Lapsi and I walked around under the trees. She was feeling frisky so we played a little game of chase, and she pranced and skipped after me as I trotted backward through the crunchy leaves.

"C'mon, Lapsi, c'mon!" I clapped my hands and, yipping happily, she bounced along with her cockeyed, arthritic gait.

In that instant, it was as though she'd never been lost or abandoned, never known cruelty or faced starvation. Nothing mattered except the warm sun on her back and the love in her heart; she was completely joyous. I carry a snapshot of the moment in my heart, and on the back of the picture I've written, "This is why we found her." Years later, I can still hear her barking, still see the color of each leaf and the sun filtering down through the maples.

Winter finally came in full force and Müsta plowed through the snow with wild abandon, making doggy angels and catching snowballs tossed high over his head. But Lapsi was less than enthusiastic. Gone were the shoveled sidewalks of the city and, confronted with drifts higher than her head, she clung to the narrow path we cleared along the walk and the tire gullies in the driveway. Although her coat and undercoat were thick and fluffy, she was like an elderly person, never warm, and would only venture far enough from the door to do her business before scooting back inside.

Rural snow was an adjustment for Kevin and me, as well. Open farm fields plus wind meant huge drifts across the roadways and the rumble of snow plows in the wee morning hours. Since we both still worked in Columbus, we left and returned home in the dark, and the snow added substantial time to our commutes. But with Mike there daily and Susie always ready to step in, weather delays were one less worry. Müsta and Lapsi were well cared for, and happy wags greeted us after the long drive home.

When the temperature dropped to the single digits, Kevin fashioned doggy boots for Lapsi: children's socks fastened together in pairs with long elastic strips stretching up over her back, connecting along her spine with a short piece of elastic. They worked, but she always did a comical high-step trying to shake them off.

Lapsi's greatest winter joy was lying by the fireplace in the evening with Müsta and the cats, all crowded on beds close to the hearth. After they'd been active all day, there was much snoring, yipping, and twitching of paws. I imagined in Lapsi's dreams she was young again, that we'd found her earlier and she'd never known hardship. She ran with Müsta, bounding across the fields, two in one motion. No arthritis or cataracts slowed her down, and she could hear the rustle of the grass as the dream bunnies fled before them. Occasionally, Lapsi's tail would thump softly against the rug.

As spring 1995 arrived, Lapsi's health started to slip, and because of her age and her dislike of trips to the vet, we decided to let nature take its course. It was a gradual process; sometimes she was her old self and other times she wandered around the house bumping into things. Her eyesight and hearing were nearly gone and she followed me closely, running into me if I abruptly stopped walking. When I sat down, she'd stand touching me with her nose. She still ate well, but her energy was fading.

On a Saturday evening in May, our friends, Steve and Mindi, were visiting and Lapsi clung to me as she always did, but she was more restless than usual. As we all sat in the living room and talked, Lapsi stood with her head in my lap and paid no attention to anyone else. While her behavior didn't seem different to me, our friends thought Lapsi had slipped a lot over the last month; weeks later, Mindi told me that when she left our house that night, she felt she wouldn't see Lapsi again.

The next morning, Müsta woke me up early and I took both dogs out in the warm spring morning. The eastern sky was a wash of pale pink and orange, painting the undersides of the soft clouds and fading off into faintest blue. It would be a perfect day. After I fed Missy, we wandered around the yard as I drank my coffee; Müsta sniffed here and there, marking his usual territory, while Lapsi did her normal duties.

Back inside, Müsta ate his breakfast but Lapsi showed no interest in her food—not a good sign. Müsta sniffed her untouched bowl, gave me his worried look, then laid down to watch Lapsi. She'd gone into the dining room by herself. I poured another cup of coffee and joined them.

In a spot of morning sunlight, Lapsi laid down for the last time. She didn't appear to be in pain and except for not eating breakfast, she gave no indication she was in her last hours. By the time Kevin woke up, she was breathing slowly and could barely raise her head. I called Susie and we agreed today was probably the day.

Kevin and Müsta went for a walk while I stayed with Lapsi, petting her gently and whispering in her ear. I wondered again about her life before, and the suffering she'd endured, surviving through strength of will and fighting each setback with quiet determination. Now, her grizzled muzzle lay limp against the toothless gums beneath, puffing out with each slow breath as she slipped away, fading beneath my hand.

Strangely, I was ready to let her go. I'd lost an old cat long before and even though he'd been very ill, I always wondered if there was something else I might have done for him. We'd done all we could for Lapsi. She lived two years, two months, and one week longer than she would have if Müsta hadn't found her. Hopefully, her time with us erased the past suffering.

Suddenly, her head came up and she tried valiantly to stand. Her bladder let go and, panting, she slumped back to the floor. I slipped a towel under her and slid her into the kitchen. Kevin and Müsta came in from the yard as Susie and the vet arrived; Lapsi's breathing was very shallow. Holding her head in my hands, I knelt to her ear.

"Sail on, old soul. Rest easy. We love you forever." Then she was gone.

Homely on the outside, with her cockeyed ears and careworn face, Lapsi's eyes had revealed a heart filled with simple love, giving everything and asking nothing. Only a twist of fate, and Müsta, had saved her from a lonely, miserable end.

The vet quietly put his things away and Susie's hand was gentle on my shoulder as they turned to leave. Our tears dropped softly on the side of Lapsi's face as we sat with her a while longer; Müsta lay with his head in Kevin's lap, saying his goodbye. Normally rowdy and ready to play on weekend mornings, he was subdued, his tennis ball forgotten out in the yard; for now, he was content to stay and comfort us.

Lapsi's body was cremated and a few days later she came home to MüFarm. In the east yard, where the sun is warm and the land slopes gently away, we buried her ashes beneath a newly planted dogwood tree, its soft pink blossoms and small leaves casting a delicate shadow. Each spring, the sturdy little tree would blossom, with Lapsi's spirit flowing up through the branches. Like the woods where we found her that cold winter day, she was guarded again by a canopy of leaves, lying in a shady spot for all time.

Old Wookie passed away about three weeks later. At age 18½, her long and winding path had taken her from birth in my small barn in northern Ohio to South Africa, to Beth's during our stay in Australia, to the Columbus condo and finally to MüFarm. For such a tiny cat she was a huge presence, with me through everything, taking all my travels and travails in stride. We buried her near Lapsi's tree in what was to become our Memory Garden, but I'll always see her there in the window, curled up, snoozing in the sun.

It's the way of dogs to understand when a pack member dies and Müsta was there for us as our tears slowly turned to fond memories and smiles. We missed Lapsi and Wookie every day and stopped at their graves on our walk each morning. Lapsi had been my shadow, always at my heel, and even though she'd hardly ever made a sound, the house was now very silent.

But Lapsi left a lasting impression on our hearts, beginning a new chapter in our life with dogs. Through our network of new friends, the world of stray, abandoned, and otherwise unwanted dogs became an important part of our lives. Rural areas have long been dumping grounds for irresponsible pet owners, and our little county shelter was constantly overwhelmed—sadly, back then many dogs were euthanized. For each one who died, alone and forgotten, their heart love went with them, their promises forever unfulfilled, their wisdom unshared. But for those who found their way to us, we made it our goal to give them a chance and help them along to new, loving families. Each success strengthened our resolve.

Odie — June 1995

Early one June morning, Müsta and I went out to the barn and found a large Coonhound sleeping on the hay.

"Well, good morning, big pup—where did you come from?" I asked, while Müsta wagged in greeting.

The dog raised his head, watching as I fed Missy, and when he jumped down from his bed, I was horrified to see he was loaded with ticks! His big, floppy ears hung heavily against his head, laden inside and out with fully engorged ticks. His legs and body were lumpy with the disgusting things.

Tick shampoo and rubber gloves were staples on Mü-Farm, and he stood very still while I lathered him up and waited for the shampoo to take effect—it must have felt so good! As the ticks dropped off, I couldn't help stepping on them and by the time I was finished the ground was covered in blood. It was totally gross but the poor dog was tick-free.

For some reason he reminded me of the dog from "Garfield," so I named him Odie. His weight and energy level were good and I guessed he was probably a local hunting dog who'd gone astray and would eventually head back home. The county shelter had no reports of a lost hound, and our neighbor down the road wasn't missing either of his hunters, so I gave Odie some food and water.

As I went about my day, puttering in the garden, Odie followed Müsta around for a while, then made himself comfortable, sleeping in front of the barn and joining the greeting committee when Kevin came home. With Lapsi gone, Kevin and I both welcomed the new boy. Toward evening, I glanced out the window and Odie was still by the barn, with something on the ground in front of him, so I went to investigate. It was a very large, very dead groundhog.

"Good Odie!" I gave him a treat from my pocket.

Groundhogs were a real problem, digging under our outbuildings and making holes out in Missy's pasture, and since we would never use poison and didn't own a gun, we'd been trying to figure out how to get rid of them. Over the next few days, Odie cleaned out the entire MüFarm groundhog population from under the corn crib and shed, their holes out in the pasture, and behind the barn. Hoping he'd stay around, we kept feeding him, but once the groundhogs were gone he vanished—I'd rid him of the nasty ticks and he repaid the favor, a very fair trade. Over time, the groundhogs returned, but we never saw Odie again. Hopefully, he found his way home. I wish we knew.

Back to one dog, MüFarm felt lonely, but it wasn't long before we filled the void. A conversation with a co-worker changed our lives and brought new joy.

CHAPTER 5
Silly, Happy Boy: 1995

Sammi

His eyes were alight with fun and a bit of the "my way or the highway" attitude. A challenge brought out the best in him and he was always ready for anything.

Christened Sampson by the family who'd raised him from a puppy, Sammi became ours when a co-worker needed to find him a new home. Sammi had been well-loved by his daddy, Randy, and Randy's two young boys, and it was hard for them to let him go.

By then, my reputation as a dog lover, rescuer, and general sucker for animals was well known among my colleagues, so I wasn't surprised one morning when Randy approached me for help. Lapsi had only been gone about six weeks and we still grieved for her, but our philosophy was, "So many dogs, so little time." Müsta was getting older but played like a pup and we knew he'd welcome a new brother.

A beautiful golden mix of Shepherd, Husky, and Lab, Sampson had a fluffy tail that curved up over his back and a deep, soft mane coming in around his neck. At just a year old, he had some growing left to do. Even with boundless pup energy he was well mannered, responded to commands, and was a fetching fool. He also loved to swim.

Randy had a bag ready with Sampson's bowls, food, and favorite toys, including a large, red, hard-plastic ball. The sadness was clear on Randy's face as we drove away, and Sampson sat watching out the window as his dad waved goodbye. A new adventure was beginning.

In keeping with the Müsta/MüFarm naming tradition, he became SammiMü but we always called him Sammi, among various other things. Kevin and I both love words and wordplay, and our pup's personalities inspired many nicknames. Sammi's personality was huge. While Müsta spoke to us with his eyes, Sammi was vocal, voicing his opinion in no uncertain terms and talking back. If SamBaloney wanted something, he let everyone know. With all his various barks and growls, Sammi developed quite a vocabulary; evidently, he liked wordplay, too.

From his first day at MüFarm, Sammi was right at home, befriending Kissa and following Müsta everywhere as the two roamed the yard and field, exploring, sniffing, and scaring up critters. Crops covered our back four acres and the seven adjacent acres—they rotated yearly between corn and soybeans—and once Sammi could be trusted to stay on the property, the two dogs spent hours each day rambling around. In the corn, they disappeared completely, following their noses in the grid of rows, somehow always emerging close to where they started. If the field was in soybeans, we followed the wanderings by watching their tails, a black and a gold, swimming in the beans. Müsta looked after his new brother and we never worried when they were out together.

While they both loved to hunt critters, Müsta just scared them up for fun; Sammi killed them. He soon discovered the many bunny nests hidden in the tall grass along the pasture fence and, short of keeping him leashed to a tie-out all day, there was no way to keep him from his hunts. It was in his blood, which paid off when it came to the groundhogs. After Odie moved on, the groundhogs returned but Sammi took care of them, waiting near the den until the groundhog poked its head out. In a blur of pounce, grab, shake, and snap, the critter would be dead. During Sammi's first summer he cleaned out every den on the property.

With the groundhogs gone, Sammi rediscovered the toys Randy had sent along, including the big red ball. About the size of a basketball, the hard plastic was thick and too heavy for him to pick up, but he'd try anyway, covering it with scratches.

"Sammi, where's Big Red?" Off he'd go to find it, then we'd bowl it across the yard and he'd push it back, creating an unusual game of fetch.

Other times, he initiated the play, amusing himself and us by chasing the ball around the yard at a dead run, pushing it with his nose and barking a unique, high-pitched sound, unlike any of his other barks. Very agile, he'd change direction to avoid hitting something or going under the pasture fence, but at times his aim was a little off. Once, he accidentally jammed the ball under our pickup truck between the muffler and the ground, and his loud, frustrated brat-bark demanded immediate attention.

"Get Big Red!" Kevin teased, as he started toward the truck.

But before Kevin got there, Sammi took action. He was too big to crawl under the truck and in frustration he started growling and tearing at the plastic trim—if Kevin hadn't been there, the poor truck would have been shredded.

Teaching Sammi to control himself was a challenge at first; his energy and curiosity demanded constant supervision. Not long after the truck incident, he nearly tore the downspout off the back of the house after he saw a toad hop into the opening. Then, a few days later, for some unknown reason he decided Lapsi's tree looked like a great toy, biting off some branches and seriously chewing the trunk before I caught him. Scolding him soundly, I cried while doctoring the little tree as I'd once tended to Lapsi. Sammi sat nearby, contrite. A short time later, the tree's remaining branches died and we were sure that was the end of it. But to our surprise, new shoots began to grow from below the wounded area. Knowing it would look odd, Kevin cut the top off to allow the new branches to grow and, just as Lapsi had rebounded from near death, her tree had a new life. Filled with her determined spirit, the quirky, cock-eyed little dogwood was a survivor. Sammi never touched the tree again—lesson learned.

To Sammi, everything was a game, including thunderstorms. One late-summer afternoon found Müsta, Sammi, and me hunkered together in the barn as the lightning moved closer. With the sliding door closed down to about two feet and Missy safely in her stall, we sat on the hay together as the rain pounded the metal roof. Müsta never worried about storms and laid with his big head on my lap, dozing. At a quick, close flash and roll of thunder, Müsta opened his eyes—but Sammi jumped up and took off running out the door. Thinking he was frightened, I started to go after him but then saw him trotting back across the yard. With each clap of thunder he repeated the game and I realized he was chasing the sound. When it stopped, back he came to wait until the next roll. Wow, a dog who actually liked thunderstorms! Throughout his life the sound of an approaching storm set him on play alert.

SamBone the Hambone constantly entertained us with his creativity, inventing new games as his personality emerged, growing to adulthood but never maturing. ("You are only young once, but you can stay immature indefinitely," as Ogden Nash wrote.) Sammi kept Müsta young, and although they got along famously, there was some brotherly competition and one-upmanship. When Kevin and I returned from work, they'd both be at the door, each carrying a stuffed toy.

But one evening, Müsta appeared alone, while Sammi frantically knocked the toy bucket around, trying to choose what to bring. Finally, he came running with two in his mouth, inspiring Kevin to write a story celebrating Sammi Two-Toy's unique creativity. What would he come up with next?

Sammi's high-intensity lifestyle demanded serious sleep, and while Müsta curled in his bed, sedate and dignified, Silly Sammi sprawled, rolling on his back with front and hind paws splayed wide, snoring away upside-down. Sometimes he slept on his side, with his head crammed against a table or chair leg in a most uncomfortable-looking posture. But trying to move him earned us a soft growl: *Can't you see I'm sleeping?*

On wet days, the towel-off game brought out his play growl as he tried to grab the towel and bat our hands away, and Sammi Snarlface emerged when the brush appeared. Grooming was not his idea of fun, but each spring, and throughout the summer, his Husky coat was a riot of loose, clumpy hair tufts.

"You look like an old mattress losing its stuffing!" I'd mutter, clipping his leash on to prevent an escape. But his ruckus was all a bluff; his snarl-smile and tail thumps gave him away, and I was not at all intimidated. He enjoyed the game as much as I did.

After his brushing, piles of Husky undercoat in a Sammi outline remained on the grass and a fierce cheeping, squawking battle ensued as the sparrows swooped down, grabbed chunks of fluff, and took off like giant, flying cotton balls. Sammi would chase them at first but quickly become bored—he wouldn't play games he couldn't win. Each fall, when storms brought down abandoned nests, there was Sammi's hair, intricately woven into the fine grass lining, while Missy's long, black mane and tail hair gave structure to the outer layers of twigs. Nothing goes to waste in the natural world.

Two shedders meant the natural world collected inside the house, too, and during the winter, dog-hair dust bunnies silently reproduced under the furniture. With the spring breeze, dust elephants awakened, crawling out from every corner and crevice, fuzzy tumbleweeds swirling around the house with Kissa in hot pursuit and me with the vacuum cleaner, trying to keep up. It was a never-ending battle. The kitchen wasn't spared, either; in our house, it's an event when there's *not* dog hair in the food!

Along with the hair was a growing collection of animal-related paraphernalia, most of it very handy even if it didn't get used very often—we never wanted to get rid of anything, just in case we might need it. Various sizes of cones, grooming tools, food and water bowls, crates, and gates ... the list goes on. Most of it we'd purchased, but arguably the most-used item of all we'd picked from the curb on a trash day years before, a plastic airline crate big enough for all but the largest dog. It fit in the car, was easy to take apart for cleaning, and became a temporary home for many animals: foster dogs, abandoned kittens, and injured wildlife including opossums, birds, and turtles. We still use it to this day.

Silly Sammi kept Müsta young, but he was 11 now, and as the winter of 1995-'96 rolled in, he began to show his age. Tennis the Menace was still his most treasured toy but while we could throw it far across the yard for Sammi, we had to tone it down for Mü. So clear were the memories of days spent endlessly running, Müsta fetching with wild abandon, never tiring out. Our winter hikes were still the long rambles we all enjoyed, but slower now as we paced ourselves. Müsta remained our happy, loving boy, but we could no longer ignore time creeping along, and it terrified us.

With spring, our trips to Alum Creek returned and the smell of the lake always perked Müsta up. We remembered the days of carefree sailing, but now our little boat sat in the shed next to the barn, forlorn and waiting for someday beyond the demands of farm chores and house remodeling. Kevin and Müsta took it out once or twice with his nephew, Eric, but with multiple animals now, I stayed home, glad that Kevin and Mü could still enjoy being on the water. Eventually our trailer broke down, ending our sailing days for good. But we couldn't part with the boat and the shed became its dry dock for many years.

Sailing or not, Müsta came alive at the beach, and the fetching competition with Sammi kept him going. Sammi was a good swimmer but not graceful like Müsta, who glided effortlessly through the water. Sammi's style was ungainly as he paddled with his head held high, breaking the surface with his front paws, splashing with each stroke and pushing the tennis ball away. Typical Sammi, he never knew when to quit—and if there were two balls in the water he tried to get them both, lunging and snapping and usually succeeding. Müsta took frequent rests on the sunny sand at water's edge but he'd bark as Sammi ran past, as if jealous of Sammi's young-dog energy, then get up to join the fun again.

SILLY, HAPPY BOY: 1995

As summer progressed, Müsta's hips became weaker and he needed a boost getting up, but once on his feet he walked fine. With pain medication he returned to his old self for a while—even up for a game of Tennis the Menace fetch—and then some blood work indicated liver trouble. The numbers had been creeping up, and we now faced the beginnings of liver failure. Determined to make his last summer glorious, we carried on with normal activities as long as he was willing, savoring each day.

The leaves turned and fell, and in Müsta's eyes I began to see a change, as if he knew something we didn't, a secret he wasn't quite ready to share. Sammi also sensed the change, giving Müsta space and toning down his play. There was no way to prepare ourselves for what was coming, but quality of life was our benchmark and we watched him closely—he would tell us when it was time.

Müsta was the one who taught us what we needed to know, making us understand that after the fight is gone, after the days of special food and medications, the nights of 2:00 a.m. dashes outside and midnight carpet cleanings, the point comes when enough is enough. First came the separation, when he'd lie by the back door, apart from us, as if he just wanted to be gone—which, of course, was what he was trying to tell us. We didn't want to believe.

As his liver worsened, his system began to fail and the secret in his eyes revealed a subtle distance as he began to turn inward. The message was unbearable, but unmistakable, stated so clearly and with such dignity: *Let me go now. It's done*. No fear, no sadness, just his simple request. Acceptance was extremely hard for me, but Kevin really struggled. For so long, Müsta was our only child, the center of our lives, but the morning came when Kevin, too, understood what he was telling us. I scheduled the house call for later in the day.

Müsta ate a little breakfast and on our walk both dogs were subdued. Sammi knew his brother was struggling and they walked slowly, side by side, Müsta's red jacket dapper against his black fur. Sammi was always such a big, rambunctious puppy, interested only in toys and play, but watching him now we saw a new side as he focused on Müsta, somehow understanding what his brother was facing. After a few minutes, Müsta's energy gave out and he laid down under the backyard lollipop maple tree, so named for its shape. It was his favorite outside place and over time he'd created a low, hollow spot between two big roots.

"It's OK, buddy, take a rest. We'll be right back," we assured him, and headed for the field with Sammi. As we walked away across the yard, Müsta's eyes didn't follow us. His journey was beginning.

After our hike we went inside but Müsta stayed out under his tree, and as I stood at the window watching him, the memories tumbled through my mind—from porky little puppy to wizened, grizzled old man, his joy filled our days. Now, he lay quietly under the tree looking out over his land, the little farm we bought mostly for him. I went outside and sat next to him. He laid his warm head on my leg and I stroked it gently, the broad, noble skull and black velvet ears, the feel of him so familiar under my hand.

"We love you, old buddy." Our eyes met. *I know, Mom.*

Kevin came outside with Sammi and we all sat together for the last time. Müsta was the light of our lives, our whole world, and very soon he would leave us. My heart could not accept it.

Later, after the vet left, we sat for a while in the cool shade, unable to believe Müsta was really gone. He'd shared long, wonderful wanderings with us, giving us way more than we ever gave him. Compassion was his guiding force, his greatest gift, and in the end, we returned it to him; he was at peace.

Sammi got up and wandered off across the yard, and that was our signal—it was late afternoon and we had a grave to dig. The site we chose was in our newly planted apple orchard in the Memory Garden, near Wookie and not far from Lapsi's tree; a perfect place for our perfect boy. He rested on a bed of fresh hay, Tennis the Menace forever between his front paws. A small lantern hung above the grave, its candle casting a peaceful glow over his stone and the freshly turned earth.

Goodbye, beautiful boy. Thank you for leading us on an adventure beyond belief, for teaching us to always be curious, compassionate, and joyful, and to live in the moment every day.

While Lapsi's loss was hard, Müsta had been with us nearly our entire married life, and the hole he left in our hearts seemed too big to ever heal. With Sammi to keep us going we carried on, but we missed Müsta constantly, his demands for playtime, the sound of his bark, his soft snoring each evening. Watching from the yard, we ached to see the black and blond tails swimming together in the beans, as Sammi now wandered the field on his own.

But Müsta would not be our last loss. Loving and committing to animals for life means eventually losing them, and moving forward is the only option.

Sammi was in charge of Dad and Mom now and took the job seriously, keeping track of everything we did. Filling Müsta's role, Sammi became our creative and social director, and on weekends his bright, questioning eyes and demanding woofs told us what he wanted: *Sammi sez a walk in the woods would be tops*, or *Sammi sez let's go to Alum Creek Lake*. He was up for any activity and brought his own style of participation, just to make sure we didn't take things too seriously.

But early 1997 was a very tough time on MüFarm. On the heels of Müsta's death, Missy lost a long struggle with laminitis, and we put her down in March. It was a terrible loss for Cindy and me. I was there at Missy's birth, and had trained and ridden her most of her early life. Like Wookie, Missy had endured my wandering 20s, and we learned and grew together. Using intuition and the advice of my horse friends, I'd trained her from the ground up, and before I ever rode her, she could move through her gaits on voice commands alone. Our bond was strong; when her deep, brown eyes met mine, the look between us conveyed instant understanding.

When Cindy bought her, Missy became a show horse and with professional training she grew into a bold, versatile competitor. With her shiny bay coat, black mane and tail, and big white forehead star, she was a looker, demanding attention and turning heads. Stepping outside the classes typical of an American Saddlebred, she excelled at everything from jumping to children's Western Pleasure and was always game for a new challenge. But outside the show ring, she

SILLY, HAPPY BOY: 1995

was the babysitter—the trainer would put her very-young daughter up in the saddle and Missy would circle the round pen quietly, content to care for her little rider.

Once back with me on MüFarm, Missy enjoyed her well-earned routine of leisurely trail rides and pasture time. Each evening found her at the gate ready for her grooming, our solitary time together, and as the sun slanted through the barn, the sounds of rustling, munching hay brought peace to us both. Our lives had intertwined for so long—I was there at her beginning, the first thing she saw when she opened her eyes, and now I would be there as her eyes closed forever.

Throughout Missy's struggle, treatment, and final decline, Sammi stuck right there with me, saying his goodbye at the end. A neighbor came with his backhoe and buried Missy near the field, below the Memory Garden; we planted a horse-chestnut tree to guard her spot, stately and beautiful and filled with her bold spirit. Sammi oversaw everything and the sense of closure brought us all comfort.

With Müsta gone and the barn empty, the farm was very lonely—we needed a buddy for Sammi. It didn't take long for one to find us.

CHAPTER 6
The World's Happiest Dog: 1997

bear

True to his breed in every sense, he was a happy-go-lucky Yellow Lab whose tail never stopped wagging unless he was in the deepest sleep. His physical condition indicated a hard life, but his eyes were filled with innocence, trust, and pure joy.

As dogs entered and left our lives I became convinced there was a purpose behind each one. Müsta had set the standard, teaching us how to train a dog and how to read and understand them through their eyes. Lapsi introduced us to the power of determination and the rewards of rescuing, showing us they all deserve a chance. Sammi was still teaching us every day, providing a zany balance to the working world. Bear's lesson would be a simple one: be happy.

After our recent losses, the Powers That Be sent us what we needed. Our local newspaper came out every Wednesday, usually with one or two pictures from the shelter, grainy black-and-whites showing pleading eyes and lost souls. Bear was different. He'd come to the shelter as a stray, wearing a filthy collar and dragging a chain, but his picture showed a ball in his grinning mouth and a brightness in his eyes, shining through whatever his past had been. We wanted him immediately. Although committed to rescue and adoption, we were Lab lovers deep inside, so Bear was the best of both worlds.

Bear was our first adoptee from the Morrow County Dog Shelter, but certainly not the last. In 1997, the shelter let the dogs go to the first person who showed up with $17, the cost of the county dog license. No contract to sign, no check to verify what kind of home the dog would get, no promise to spay or neuter. Those who weren't quickly adopted were euthanized. The shelter has come a long way since then.

Since we worked full time, I gave my $17 to my neighbor, Susie, and she picked him up, then took him for his shots and a check-up at the veterinary clinic where she worked. Susie told me later that the minute she saw him she knew he had heartworms; he was very thin and his dull, brittle coat said it all. The infestation was bad, the treatment would be difficult, and there was a good chance he might not survive. But when we visited him at the clinic that night, even in his sorry state of health he got all wiggly, climbing on us as we sat on the floor.

An English Lab, Bear was square and solid, with a head even broader than Müsta's; the vet lovingly called him a classic blockhead. His coat was very light, the hairs tipped with brown—our toasted-marshmallow boy—but he was dirty to the skin and we promised him a nice bath and grooming once his treatment was finished.

His teeth were so bad it was hard to even guess his age. His lower-right canine was no more than a nub and the lower-front teeth were all but gone—clearly, his care had been non-existent. Possibly a former puppy-mill stud, he was intact and probably spent his days chewing on his chain. But in spite of his past, and all through the heartworm treatment and neutering surgery, his personality never changed. His eyes always said, *OK, whatever's next, I'll love it!*

Bear wasn't housebroken so on his first day home we crated him and Susie stopped by to take him out while Kevin and I were at work. But when we got home that evening, we were greeted at the door by both Sammi and a grinning Bear; the gate on the large crate was still firmly latched. Kevin then built a sturdy pen in the basement—from which Houdini-dog promptly escaped.

Fortunately, Bear caught on to housebreaking and was soon free to sleep the day away with Sammi. Although Sammi could be guarded around other dogs, Bear was so laid-back there was no pack competition and they bonded easily, sharing the toys and beds. In contrast to Sammi's intensity,

Bear was content to ramble around and bask in everyone's love. They were a perfect balance.

Bear loved everything that made a Lab a Lab, carrying his ball everywhere and always on the hunt for a place to swim. During his first MüFarm summer, he discovered that a jaunt with Sammi across the field brought him to Owl Creek, and on hot days he'd help himself to a quick cool-down. While the creek ran across the back of our property, it was outside of our acreage so was technically off limits. In the summer when the water was low it was also very muddy, turning our marshmallow boy into a chocolate Lab.

To keep the peace with the neighbors, and to keep both dogs clean and cool, we bought a large plastic kiddie pool. But for some reason they wouldn't step over the sides, so they became the only dogs for miles around with their own in-ground pool. Kevin picked a spot near the corn crib, dug a big round hole, and sank the pool in at ground level. From then on we couldn't keep them out of it. The pool was big enough for them both to jump in and lie down, causing the water to overflow, so we spent a lot of time refilling—another excuse for a Silly Sammi game. A running hose was an open invitation and he'd snap at the water, splashing it everywhere, then grab the hose and race around the yard, with Bear close behind.

During the hot, dry weather the pool was also popular with frogs and toads; to give them easy access we found a slab of wood, stripped the bark off, and we called it, then and forever after, the Frog Log. They basked on it during the day, hid under it at night, and used it as a launching pad back to land. Of course, a Lab can no more resist a stick than a ball, so Sammi and Bear were constantly stealing the log, carrying it around and then leaving it somewhere for us to retrieve. Bear, especially, was enamored with it, pawing at it in the water until he got a good grip and then carrying it away like a prize, the weight of the log cocking his head to an angle. No matter what he did he always wore his patented Bear Smile, as if perpetually pleased with himself and with life in general.

Whether in the house or somewhere outside, we seldom saw one dog without the other, and they kept us constantly amused.

"Aren't pupz great?" Kevin observed. "They keep us from ever having to grow up and do all the serious parent things human children require."

Calling them the pupz was one of our many silly ways. Kevin decided that since some people used "dog" as a derogatory term, we should call them "pupz"—with a "z" to be unique—and it became part of our vocabulary. As a type-A personality, I tend to be tightly wound, and when the demands of work, the 90-minute round-trip drive, and other daily details weighed on me, all it took was a field hike or fetch session to whack things back into perspective. Everything the pupz did was driven by a first-time, every-time zeal, and a dose of silliness here and there kept us all focused on what really mattered.

Sammi was now Daddy's boy. While he loved us both, he really attached himself to Kevin, sensing his struggle over the loss of Müsta. Wherever Kevin was in the house or yard, Sammi wasn't far away, ready to help with any chore.

The fence surrounding the horse pasture desperately needed replacing, and the summer '98 project was new wooden posts and a woven wire fence. The old fencing was cleared away and on weekend mornings, Kevin would load the wheelbarrow with a manual post-hole digger, a bag of concrete, gravel, a water container, and several new wooden posts.

Sammi soon learned this meant hours of fun, "supervising." His essential tool for any project was a tennis ball and he trotted along after Kevin, waiting for the wheelbarrow to stop and the digging to begin.

Every Sammi game had a twist, including fetch. The post hole was the perfect size for a tennis ball so Sammi would drop it in, then Kevin would dig the ball out, throw it, and try to get some serious work done before Sammi ran back for more. The ground under our property was very rocky, so digging rocks, dirt, and ball out of each hole slowed the project considerably. But the game was so much fun neither of them cared, and Kevin's laughter, combined with Sammi's joyous barks, floated into the summer sunshine. Eventually, the fence was complete and Sammi had to find something new to supervise. Fortunately, there was always a project.

Truck trips became a favorite, whether it was runs to the store for project supplies or Monday night pizza pick-up, and the extended cab, with the jump seats flipped up, was Sammi's spot. He loved the truck, even when there were no trips to take, and during outdoor chores, he'd follow us around the yard until he got bored, and then sit by the truck door barking until we opened up. In our summertime Sammi memories, he's curled up on the seat with the doors open and the Cleveland Indians game on the radio, supervising as we go about our activities.

THE WORLD'S HAPPIEST DOG: 1997

On weekends, for a change of scenery and a break from chores, we'd often head to Mount Gilead State Park, a nearby hiking and pup-swimming destination with wonderful trails winding up into the woods, following the shallow river, then circling the lake below. Stands of old trees sheltered a variety of wildlife and we'd sometimes see a bald eagle cruising high above the lake, and turtles basking on fallen logs. A little oasis amidst a desert of dry, rolling farmland, the park was a hidden gem, never crowded, and beautiful any time of year.

The pupz loved roaming through the trees, bounding up and down the steep trails, and splashing in the river. Intrepid, curious Sammi was always in the lead in a constant hurry to see what was next, while Bear followed at his own pace, ambling along, looking here and sniffing there to be sure he didn't miss anything. After a peaceful hour or two we'd turn to head home, clipping on the pupz' leashes and sparking a favorite Sammi game: he'd grab the leash, shaking his head while I tugged gently.

"Fish on a line! Fish on a line! Mom caught a big fish!" I'd sing.

After a minute of play-growl nonsense he'd drop the leash and carry on with his walk, content he'd made us laugh.

Sammi's "a game for every occasion" attitude even made exercising a joy. Each morning as Kevin unrolled his mat and strapped on his ankle weights, Sammi would appear with a toy, usually what we called the "Brain Ball."

"No, Dad's busy exercising," Kevin teased.

Undeterred, Sammi would drop the ball on Kevin's face or chest, demanding a throw. As a last resort, he'd push the toy between Kevin's legs—he would not be ignored—and as the exercise routine devolved into laughing, barking chaos it was impossible to tell who was having more fun.

The Brain Ball wasn't really a brain; in the catalog they were called Flower Balls. Embossed with a nubby pattern, the soft, flexible, latex squeaky balls came in several different colors and two sizes. Sammi preferred the baseball-sized ones and always kept several close by, so I bought them in bulk, 12 to a box. Bear loved anything squeaky and chose the larger, softball-sized version, holding one squished in his mouth like a big orange or yellow smile, grinning and wagging. Bear's mission in life was to make us laugh, and he was very good at it.

The Sammi and Bear years were so amusing! The canine Odd Couple, each had specific preferences and quirks, but they got along so well. Of course, Bear got along with everyone. In everything we did Sammi was high energy while Bear went along for the ride.

A shout of "Car ride!" set both tails wagging and it didn't matter where we went or whether we took the truck or the car. In the back, Bear always sat on the right side, happy to watch the world go by, while navigator Sammi was behind the driver, constantly looking out the front window, cramming himself between the door post and headrest, with his head on the driver's left shoulder. Rain and windshield wipers would start a Sammi frenzy as he bobbed his head back and forth, following the motion, while highway rumble strips sent him diving for the floor, tipping his head and barking; the drive-through car wash was total madness. Unflappable Bear slept soundly through it all.

Any fast movement set Sammi off. One memorable day I returned from work to find the first floor in total disarray: the fireplace doors were open, tools scattered around the hearth, rugs crumpled in corners, and black marks on the walls and windows. Sammi and Bear sat panting in the center of the wreck, staring up at the corner cupboard in the dining room. Perched on top was one very tired, very sooty bird. Birds had come down the chimney before so we always kept the glass fireplace doors closed, but in his excitement Sammi must have hit the latch. Birds held no interest for him outside, but inside the house was another thing entirely.

After releasing the bird, I fed the pupz and took them for a field hike until Kevin got home—he'd get a laugh out of the mess and no way was I going to clean it up all by myself! Later, as we scrubbed away, we pictured the fun they must have had, first spying the bird flapping inside the fireplace and then following its crazed darting through the rooms as it searched frantically for an escape. It was one of the few times Bear got excited about something other than food or a ball. Incredibly, nothing was broken, and the next day we ordered the installation of a bird-proof chimney cap. Every day was an adventure.

Bear was so easy, content to be his own sweet self, to bask in the love of his people and anyone else who came by. His ranked list of favorite things was eating, playing ball, and being petted. If ever a dog wore his heart on his sleeve it was Bear, open and innocent, willing to trust anyone. He never met a stranger. Sammi loved people, too, but was more reserved, preferring older kids or adults, who were more likely to play a serious game of fetch. With Sammi, it was always ball play first and everything else second.

Although Bear belonged to us completely, his love and trust of people tempted him to take off and follow others, especially children. At the sound of a child's voice or laughter he'd immediately come to attention, grab the nearest toy or stick, and take off, wagging madly. On summer Sundays, when the Baptist church held services, the children would play in the churchyard afterward and the running, shrieking kids were a Bear magnet.

After services one especially beautiful day, the congregation gathered in the church basement for their meal, leaving the door open for fresh air. Bear could also never resist food so he boldly trotted across the road and down the basement steps to invite himself to the party. Retrieving our wayward child, we found him shamelessly begging from the children at the table. It's our favorite Bear memory.

Over our years on MüFarm, the church congregation became family to us. When it was established in 1843, the tiny church and its handful of members had anchored the town of Penlan, along with a general store/post office (now our next-door neighbor's house) and schoolhouse (our barn). While we never became part of the congregation, we considered it our church. Their infrequent services meant the building stood empty much of the time, leaving it vulnerable to vandalism. We kept watch to be sure no monkey business took place and called one of the deacons or the sheriff, if necessary. It was a treasured relationship.

THE WORLD'S HAPPIEST DOG: 1997

Along with our rescue/adoption activities, we also volunteered with the Humane Society of Morrow County, mostly at fundraisers. Each fall, the Ohio Gourd Society held its annual festival at the Morrow County Fairgrounds and it was quite the event as gourd growers and lovers came from all over the state for two days of gourd madness, culminating with the crowning of the gourd king and queen and a parade. The humane society always set up a booth with dog-related items for sale and a big cast-iron pot of homemade ham and bean soup simmering over an open fire. I volunteered at the booth, and Bear was my sidekick, sitting out in front, smiling and wagging, making sure no one passed by without stopping. People waiting in the soup line made a big fuss over him.

One year, we entered him in the festival parade and instead of making him walk, we fitted out our two-wheeled garden cart with crepe paper and a hanging sign: "BearBear, the Gourd King." Kevin pulled that silly cart through the entire parade as Bear sat grinning, certain all the onlookers were clapping and cheering just for him.

As the years passed, our pupz' habits and quirks became part of daily life, and any deviation was immediately suspect. About a year after Bear joined us, Sammi began losing muscle tone in his face and head and went off his food. The diagnosis was masticatory muscle myositis, an autoimmune disease affecting the jaw and facial muscles. I researched the condition and was terrified to learn how progressive and fatal it could be. The available treatment was an aggressive dose of prednisone administered over several months, with the dose tapering down as the condition stabilized. Any muscle tone already lost was gone for good, so stopping the progression was critical. We began the treatment and hoped for the best.

Sammi tolerated it well, but the high dose of pred suppressed his entire immune system so we watched him closely; sure enough, an infection developed, swelling his right elbow to the point where it was hard for him to lie down. We started antibiotics but one night he was very uncomfortable, pacing around in the kitchen, trying to find a way to sleep. I couldn't sleep either so went downstairs, desperate to help him somehow.

"Is my poor Sammi so tired?" I sat on the floor and he laid down against me; when his elbow hit the floor, the terrible swollen spot burst open. I applied a warm, damp towel and gentle pressure, which gave him instant relief as the fluid drained away. He fell asleep and I stayed with him until the swelling was gone. The hole in his elbow was about a quarter-inch in diameter and would need to be kept clean while it healed, so I wrapped it with gauze for the rest of the night; we'd figure something out in the morning.

The next day, the first thing we tried was covering the gauze with sticky, stretchy Vet Wrap. It worked for about 10 minutes before it slid down his leg. Obviously, standard bandages and wraps weren't going to work. Even with his medications and the relative discomfort of his condition, there was no way he would rest or stay in one place; our energy boy was always on the move. When he was up and about the elbow stayed clean, but it needed protection when he laid down.

From my years of sewing I was used to creating makeshift solutions to various problems and had a trunk full of fabric scraps and sundries. My sister Beth and I always said, "Don't ever challenge an engineer's daughter," because we'd always come up with a solution, and even if it looked funky, it would work! Digging out Müsta's old sailing life vest, I sacrificed one of my bras and cut out one of the cups. Using two strips of elastic, I attached the cup to the vest, adjusting it to hang just below Sammi's elbow joint. The elastic allowed the cup to move with his leg but snug up against the elbow when he laid down. It was indeed funky-looking, but Sammi tolerated it well and within two weeks the wound was healed.

After several months of prednisone, the myositis progression seemed to have stopped, Sammi was eating normally, and there appeared to be no further loss of muscle. We weaned him off the steroid and while his face was never the same, the muscle strength returned. Our boy had come through; Silly Sammi was back. Sammi and Bear were once again a happy pair and MüFarm returned to normal—for a while, anyway.

CHAPTER 7
Soulmates: 2000

red

My heart broke for him when I saw his condition, but his eyes held me, reflecting the love he so desperately wanted to give, and the uncertainty of a dog mistreated and terribly neglected. The shadow of doubt hung there like a curtain with all the unspeakable things he'd endured hidden behind it. I made up my mind to change it all for him, forever.

Admittedly, Kevin and I are not great at fostering since we wanted to keep them all. Through the humane society and the dog shelter we'd taken in puppies—they're pretty easy to place and never stayed around long—but we were saps for the old ones and neglect cases.

In mid-February 2000, a three-week spell of extreme cold and snow had just ended when the dog warden called, asking if we could take in a foster since the shelter was full. The dog had spent his rescue night in the warmth of the shelter and when I went to get him, he jumped up against me, simply wanting to belong to someone. I was in trouble. My head said, he's a foster, remember? But in my heart he was already mine, and I'd named him Red.

No pure breeding showed in the line of his jaw or the set of his ears—he was what I fondly refer to as a rag-bag dog. Matted clumps hung from his filthy coat and he was unbearably thin; the outline of his ribs showed clearly and his spine stuck up in little knobs all the way to his tail. To most people he probably didn't look like much: a medium-sized, red-brown dog with longish fur and a little white sprinkled around his muzzle. His face was handsome in a way only a dog lover could appreciate: broad in the forehead and tapering toward a snout a little too long and narrow. His ears stuck out then flopped down, framing full, deep reddish-brown eyes ringed with black lids; a thin black line trailed away from the outside corners. They were eyes that wore a perpetually questioning look, as if in the back of his soul he was never really sure of anything.

Our new dog warden was working hard to improve conditions at the shelter and we were part of a network of foster homes for those in need of more intense care. The warden shared what he could about Red's case: he was found tied outside in the bitter cold with no food or water. It was obvious he'd been neglected for quite some time.

After a bath Red looked much better, and grooming efforts through the first week stripped out piles of old undercoat and tangled burrs. But even clean and groomed his dull, dry coat indicated heartworms, and Red's first vet visit revealed a bad infestation, along with intestinal worms. Leaving him for the treatment was very hard. Our bond had already begun, and from inside the kennel bars his ears drooped, and his resigned eyes followed me out the door. He was being abandoned yet again.

"I promise I'll be back!" I tried to reassure him.

But what if he didn't survive the treatment? He'd die all alone without me there with him at his end. The vet promised to call me if he thought Red wasn't going to make it.

Red came through. With good care and regular food his health steadily improved and during his first several weeks back home, I saw the beginnings of the quiet determination that would impress me throughout his life. He reminded me of Lapsi.

Apparently, he'd never been in a house before; the few stairs up to our back porch stumped him and he wasn't housebroken, so at first we crated him at night and while we were at work. It was hard keeping him in the crate so much, but he never barked or resisted, content to have a full tummy and a warm, dry place to sleep. Unlike Lapsi, Red was young and rebounded quickly, joining the pack on field walks and learning the routine of MüFarm. With regular grooming, his coat became a beautiful auburn, the long hairs tipped in black, with thick, tan fluff underneath. Sturdy and square in the body, his legs supported him at the four corners and his long tail, with wonderful feathers, rippled like a flag when he ran.

Of course, he was supposed to be a foster dog and once he was housebroken and back to health, I made a few half-hearted attempts to place him. *Maybe*, I thought, if I found someone who *really* fell in love with him, I could let him go. Within my network of friends and co-workers, two families showed interest, but at one home Red growled at the resident dog and the other family said he was too big. Secretly relieved, I stopped looking. Even though he'd only been with us a short time, we already loved him and couldn't imagine MüFarm without him. Red was home.

Watching new ones settle in and find their place in the pack is always interesting. Sammi was top dog and Bear cared nothing about pecking order, so Red eased into the family, bonding especially with me. Like Lapsi, he became my shadow, always at my heel, and as we moved through the first several months I began to observe the results of his past treatment.

Constant piles of scrap drywall, insulation, and lumber followed us from room to room as our house remodeling continued. One day while cleaning up, I picked up a length of 2x4 to take it outside. As usual, Red was right there with me and as I turned around with the board in my hand, he fell to the floor, cowering, his eyes filled with fear: *Please don't hit me!* I crumpled next to him, petting and soothing until his trembling slowly subsided.

"I promise, no one will ever hurt you again, *ever!*" I whispered. To think anyone could have abused this gentle dog made my whole being ache.

Loud noises also upset him; a cupboard door shut too hard or a pan lid dropped on the floor made him jump and run away, looking back to see if he was being chased. Fear like that was not overcome easily. It would be a long time, if ever, before he felt totally secure.

As the months went by, Red and I developed an almost spiritual relationship—in his deep, penetrating gaze was the knowledge we had somehow known each other before. I love all dogs but my connection with Red was different. If a dog and a human could be soulmates, Red was mine and I was his.

One evening during our first winter together, I sat pensively on the floor next to the fireplace and he came and snuggled against my side. With my arm around him, he leaned more firmly into me, resting his head on my shoulder: *What's wrong, Mom? I'll make it better.* We sat for a long time and his head grew heavy as he dozed, sliding slowly down my arm into my lap.

Anytime I was sick, Dr. Red stayed close as I rested on the couch or bed, keeping watch until I was back on my feet. Each morning when I left for work his eyes asked if I was coming back, and he was always there waiting at the end of the day.

Through their bond of past turmoil and hardship, Red and Bear also developed a special affection for each other. Often, as I watched them together, I imagined their lives before: Red, doomed to die alone on a bitter-cold night, and Bear, living on a chain, wanting so desperately to share his joy. MüFarm was their forever-safe place.

Despite having been city kids all our lives, Kevin and I found that rural living suited us well. Since we both still worked in Columbus, we stepped between worlds daily and agreed the biggest benefit of rural life was no traffic. After exiting the freeway the roads were quiet, and at home on our little corner, if two cars drove by within the same 10 minutes, we looked to see what was going on. During spring and fall, all manner of farming equipment would emerge, so we got used to cruising along the roads at a few miles per hour. Narrow roads and deep ditches meant passing wasn't an option.

One drawback of country living was the ticks. Dogs and warm weather meant we were constantly on alert for the crawlies and while they were easy to spot on Sammi and Bear, Red's dark coat gave them good camouflage. During our early years with Müsta and Lapsi, the tick skirmishes were light. But now we faced the heavy artillery, and Kevin's creative abilities allowed us to have a little fun as we did battle. "Morrow County Tick-quila" appeared in every room: fancy, wooden-topped glass jars filled with rubbing alcohol, with dead ticks—instead of a worm—at the bottom.

But the biggest negative around MüFarm was the gunfire. Many of our neighbors hunted—even off-season target shooting was common—and although Sammi loved thunder, we discovered early on that he hated gunfire. For some reason, neither guns nor thunder bothered Red, and Bear paid no attention, but as July 4, 2000, approached we had no idea what to expect from any of them.

As bold as Müsta was, he didn't like fireworks and they terrified poor Lapsi, so we never celebrated Independence Day, even after they were gone. But for our new neighbor to the south, party time started before the 4th with the big, powerful stuff. Bear cowered by the back door so we put him in the basement with Kissa and Mouse, our new housecat. Red totally surprised me, going about his business outside, raising his head as each boom went off but otherwise ignoring the fireworks.

Sammi, on the other hand, went nuts! To him, the noise was obviously different from gunfire and he wanted to chase the fireworks like he did with thunder. With Bear safely inside, we decided to celebrate the 4th too, so Kevin bought a small package of bottle rockets, nothing loud or fancy but enough to keep Sammi from chasing onto the neighbor's property.

At the top of Turner Trail, we set our launcher pointed down toward the field. As Kevin prepared to light the first one I held Sammi back, releasing him only after the rocket was safely in the air. It was insanity! Barking like a maniac, Sammi bolted across the field until the rocket disappeared into the soybeans, then came tearing back to stick his nose in the top of the bottle. *More, Dad, more! More! More!* Red chased Sammi half-heartedly for a while, but he was mostly content to sit near me and watch the fun. When the rockets finally ran out, a panting Sammi headed straight for the pup pool. Life with him was a never-ending party.

Whether a workday or weekend, routines—both pup and human—defined everything on MüFarm. Kevin's Finnish-ness demanded morning coffee before anything else (except letting the pupz out) and once we were fueled up and the guys were fed, we'd get down to all the other silly stuff.

Each morning, Kevin would fold up squares of toilet paper, dampen them, and clean the pupz' eyes, singing a little song to each, accompanied by much tail wagging. From the shower upstairs I'd hear the chaos of Kevin's morning exercises, then all the pupz would follow me to the kitchen. When the blender came out, there was a smoothie line-up behind me.

After plopping in some yogurt I'd add fruit, giving each pup a sliver of pineapple and a small chunk of banana and strawberry. Bear ate anything that didn't eat him first, but he especially liked strawberries. Sammi and Red didn't care for banana, but they ate it to keep Bear from getting it all. While prunes didn't go into the smoothies, Kevin ate several with breakfast and he'd toss one to each pup. Red and Bear always begged for more, but not Sammi—he'd catch it in his mouth, roll it around, then "blop" it out on the floor, beginning yet another Sammi game. Even though he wouldn't eat it, he'd lie on the floor, guarding it.

"I'm gonna get it!" Kevin would playfully reach for the prune and Sammi would play-snarl, grabbing the prune and rolling it around again in his mouth before blopping it back out.

After a few minutes he'd finally eat it. Not because he wanted to; he just didn't want anyone else to have it. But one morning he left it. Somehow, both Red and Bear missed it, and the prune sat there all day. When I came home from work and saw a round, brown thing on the floor, I assumed someone left me a little present.

Fortunately, we never had any serious food fights. Our guys all got along well but whenever we added a pup, or when one passed away, we were on watch as the pack dynamics and mealtime hierarchy shifted. Bear understood Sammi was alpha, but once Red began to feel secure, Sammi felt challenged. After some early skirmishes Red deferred, and even when Sammi did assert himself it was more of a "playground bully" type of dominance rather than real aggression.

But try as we did, they never learned to sit patiently for their food and mealtime was always energized. If they were all in the house as I readied the bowls, Sammi would make sure everyone waited in their proper place. If they were outside, Sammi would sit, glued to the screen door, after chasing the others off the back porch. Red would sit forlornly in the yard while Bear, in his excitement, would run circles around the house. With bowls finally down, peace reigned for a few minutes while the happy sound of clinking collar tags filled the kitchen.

By this time, we were officially crazy dog people—our pupz were our whole world and almost everything we did was with, or for, them. Parties at holidays and birthdays were a must. Christmas meant a trip to the Goodwill store for inexpensive stuffed toys, and an online order for another box of Brain Balls. Party-boy Sammi loved packages, and after the tree was decorated he'd lie next to it, guarding the presents until Christmas Eve. Then, a riot would ensue as the odds and ends of gift paper and brown paper bags were ripped away; the living room floor became a sea of toys and shredded paper.

For birthdays, we used their "gotcha" date or made a best guess; it didn't really matter as long as we gave each of them a party once a year. Out came the official Birthday Crown, and Kevin would make a little cake out of canned dog food, topping it with a dab of sour cream and a candle. The cake was shared, cards and presents opened, and I'm not sure whether it meant more to them or to us.

Pup gifts had to be chosen carefully, since each showed a definite toy preference. Müsta had loved the really big ones—a giant Sea World Shamu was his favorite—while Sammi liked medium-sized toys he could cram into his mouth two or three at a time. Bear was such a ball boy he loved even the stuffed plush ones; a favorite was a life-sized soccer ball and he was always begging for a game. But he also liked smaller toys: Pink Pig and Penelope Pineapple were his special ones. Red used the toys mostly as pillows, and one Christmas a three-foot alligator became his favorite. Green Gator was carried from room to room, slept on, and even taken outside. I mended it many times before it finally fell apart.

Red also enjoyed Tug o' War with Bear, and whatever they were pulling usually ended up in pieces. While Bear had the Lab soft-mouth, his jaws were very strong and no one, pup or human, could beat him at Tug o' War. Our pup towels never lasted long, either, since dry-off time always turned into a tugging game, and while Sammi and Red gave in, Bear would make off with his prize, dragging the towel behind him and tripping on it.

Oddly, none of the pupz tore the plush toys apart for fun, and some of them, like Pink Pig, hung around for years, surviving multiple journeys through the wash. Pink Pig went nearly everywhere with In-and-Out Bear, but since he was easily distracted by scents and critters, many times the toy wouldn't make it back in the house. One tragic day, Pink Pig went outside and didn't return. We hunted for her each time we went for a walk, but she was nowhere to be found. Bear searched the toy bucket for several days, looking for his little pal, but finally gave up.

"I told you if you left Pink Pig outside the aliens would get her," I teased. His sweet, innocent eyes smiled back, then he proceeded to take another toy from the bucket and carry it outside.

Outside things made their way in as well: sticks, nasty old tennis balls lost in the pasture for ages, anything that caught Bear's fancy. Once, he trotted proudly into the kitchen with one of my muddy garden gloves, stolen from my tool bucket. He was so pleased with himself I couldn't scold him.

"It's a good thing you're so cute," I told him all the time. "You can get away with a lot of stuff when you're cute." He'd grin in agreement.

Chores on MüFarm changed with the seasons, always involving full-pack participation—twice the time, but twice the fun. Snow shoveling was raucous, with Sammi burying his Brain Balls in the drifts and then digging them out, and Bear and Red catching snowballs thrown high overhead. Spring yard cleanup saw piles of sticks for them to get into and they'd pull them out of the garden cart as fast as we picked them up. Summer mowing meant finding a shady spot to lie down and supervise as I looped around on the lawn tractor.

But fall leaf raking was the favorite activity and with the old maples in front, the fun was never-ending. The prevailing southwest wind piled the leaves in the north end of the yard where a slope ran down toward the pasture, a perfect spot for three nutty pupz, two nutty people, and a Brain Ball or two or three.

Kevin would give the balls a squeak, toss them up, and watch them drop deep into the pile. The pupz would dive in, digging frantically with waving tails. Of course, they all wanted the same ball (even though there were several), and whoever found the first one began the chase, racing around the yard, through the leaves, and up and down the hill, squeaking the ball madly, wild with the zoomies. Through it all we tried to continue raking but spent more time laughing and watching all our hard work go scattering around the yard. Finally, they'd all collapse in the pile, panting, their coat colors blending with the leaves. Sitting down with them was an open invitation and they'd pile on, rolling around and begging for more play—except for Red, who was happy to sit with me in the fall sunshine, heart to heart and fully content.

The last animal-link to our early married life came to an end when Kissa passed away. She'd always been a quiet cat, but in late January 2002, she became more vocal, especially at night, trying to tell me something. The vet found nothing wrong and she was eating and using her litter box normally; she was just wearing out. I woke early one morning with the feeling something wasn't right—Kissa wasn't in her usual spot on the bed. Red followed me through the house and in our first-floor bathroom, we found her huddled in the corner near the heat register. I sat and gently lifted her into my lap. She gave a mournful meow and then she was gone.

Being with our pets when they pass has always been important to me and Red sat with me as I held Kissa and remembered. She was about 18 years old, so she'd been with us a long time and was a fixture in our lives. From humble beginnings at the Sydney RSPCA, jetting halfway around the world to our condo and then finally to MüFarm, she was as well-traveled as Wookie. Notes and pictures sent to the RSPCA over the years had kept them current on Kissa's adventures—shelter work is rewarding but emotionally draining and I'd wanted them to know that, thanks to their dedication, one of their kitties was enjoying a long and interesting life on the other side of the world. After we buried Kissa next to Wookie in the Memory Garden, I sent one last note to the shelter.

Writing the note triggered years of memories. I thought of all our critters and the chance encounters as their lives crossed ours. In the beginning, we were set on having only Labrador Retrievers, so much did we love the breed. But with Lapsi's rescue, Müsta changed us through his compassion, opening our eyes to the joy of loving castaways, the fun of knowing them, observing their differences, and learning their secret wisdom. Whether a cat or dog, a purebred or muttly mix, their hearts, we discovered, are all the same.

With our interior remodeling projects mostly completed, we started tearing stuff up outside, and nothing piques rural folks' curiosity like the delivery of a huge load of construction materials. In spring 2002, after we tore out and moved the old front door, several neighbors couldn't stand the suspense and stopped by to see what those city folk were up to now. Kevin had designed a combination front porch, three-season room, and shade arbor for the west and south sides of the house, and construction was about to begin.

Worked into the design of the shade-arbor deck was an accessible ramp, which would eventually come in handy for everything from carts of firewood to elderly pupz. The three-season room wrapped around the corner of the house, surrounded by a catwalk that connected the west porch and south shade arbor; a railing ran all the way around. At the two angled corners were open spots in the railing where the pupz could lie on the catwalk, observe the yard, then jump off when they saw something interesting.

They all loved the jump-off spots. Like the prow of a ship, the elevated vantage point gave a commanding position above it all with a clear view of their property and the road, church, and farm acreage to the west. The jump-offs became a favorite place for photographs, their faces framed by the heavy, upright timbers and the railings on either side. Sammi spent many summer afternoons laying out at the point, one paw casually draped over the edge of the porch, gazing dreamily out across his yard. Pupz came into our lives and then left us, but the jump-off spots remained, a permanent thread weaving the memories of our pack together through time.

And in between chores, we enjoyed the porch, too. Nothing but hostas would grow in the deep shade and they covered the front yard, hugging the edge of the porch. The shade and prevailing southwest breeze cooled even the hottest days, and many evenings found us in the three-season room, sitting on the glider under the wind chimes, enjoying a glass of wine as the sun danced through the trees, dappling the gardens.

With the chaos of another construction project completed, we looked forward to a quiet fall and winter. But suddenly, I lost my design firm job that I loved so much. It wasn't a total surprise. Several recent management changes had caused upheaval and it wasn't the same fun, creative place—many of my colleagues were already gone, some by their own choice and some not. But I was still devastated. After nearly 18 years, I was proud of the career I'd built and the library I created. Leaving the office the last day was difficult, but with resolve, I took with me everything I'd learned and moved forward. Thanks to my network of animal lovers, I stayed in touch with many of my former colleagues and the news of my job search spread.

Financially, it was probably the worst possible time for me to buy another horse. But Missy had been gone 5 years, I missed having a horse, and animals rarely came into our lives at opportune moments, anyway. Susie Baird went with me to meet Gunner, a beautiful Arab/Saddlebred cross—chestnut with a big, white blaze—and as he trotted toward us up the barn aisle, Susie leaned in and whispered: "Oh, you're a goner!" Gunner came home to MüFarm several weeks before Thanksgiving.

It was clear right away that none of the pupz had ever been around horses—they were very curious and wary, but they accepted their huge new brother. Gunner hadn't been around dogs, either, and at first didn't like having them in his pasture. Red and Sammi took the hint and steered clear, but since Bear loved everyone, he was sure everyone loved him. There were a few close calls in the beginning as Gunner chased poor, bewildered Bear out underneath the gate. Eventually, a truce was worked out as everyone got used to one another, and Gunner grew to enjoy the company as he grazed.

By late fall, Gunner had become comfortable in his new home, and I returned to the Penlan Park trail rides I'd enjoyed with Missy and Müsta. Gunner's previous life as a pampered show horse meant he was unprepared for the sights and sounds of the woods; snapping sticks and the pupz popping in and out of the undergrowth startled him at first. But as his trust in me grew, he relaxed and learned the fun of following the pack—until we got to the creek. While the pupz charged right in, running through the water and cooling off, Gunner froze and would go no further: *Show horses do not step in water!* He was curious but cautious, and with each trail ride he became bolder, venturing a bit closer to the creek as I let him take his time, building his confidence. The trail continued on across the creek and the pupz always ran ahead, stopping to demand: *Aren't you coming, too?*

At this point, I'd usually call the guys back and turn Gunner around, but the day came when I could feel he was ready to go on and the pack sensed it, too. We all stood for a moment as Gunner made his decision, relaxed, and stepped tentatively into the creek. It was a milestone for us all. Gunner's trust in me, his self-confidence, and his security within the pack came together, and now he could safely go wherever the pupz went.

One evening, while leading Gunner in across the pasture, something strange-looking caught my eye. In the tall grass next to the fence was Bear's long-lost Pink Pig! Reaching down, I pulled the toy free from the grass and weeds tangled around it. Pink Pig was in a sorry state. Mostly faded from the sun on the front side, the back was still pink but very dirty—she'd been outside a long time. It would take multiple washings before she even began to look clean but I brought her in, hiding her from Bear until she was presentable, and then slipped her back into the toy bucket. It didn't take Bear long to find her. His eyes lit up as he pranced around the house with his old pal in his mouth, then he promptly took her outside again.

Penelope Pineapple met a similar fate. She'd disappeared soon after Pink Pig, and while we'd hunted high and low, it seemed she was lost forever. Not long before Bear died, Kevin was out along the east fence-line down near the spring, collecting rocks in the wheelbarrow. There among the cattails was Bear's precious toy, moss and muck clinging to her fur. Kevin tossed her in the wheelbarrow. Penelope was in worse shape than Pink Pig, and it took three or four washings before she was recognizable, but Bear was happy to have her back. No matter how long his beloved toys were gone, he always remembered them.

Bear took everything in stride, not worrying much about anything, and we learned to roll with the ups and downs, as well. Missing toys and various injuries and ailments were common, so when Bear one day presented us with a big, fat ear hematoma, we knew what we were in for; we'd been through one or two with Müsta. Drained and stitched up, Bear wore the big plastic Cone of Shame, but for the first few days we were constantly rewrapping his ear. Even with the cone, our escape artist was a master at working his ear flap out of the bandage. And, being the klutz he was, Basher Bear crashed into the door frames, our legs, the other pupz, and anything else blocked from his line of sight. By the time the ear was healed and unwrapped for good, the cone was bent, cracked, and totally trashed.

We also flowed along with the never-ending stream of beds, blankets, towels, and toys that piled up each week. In the summer, mass washings were followed by herds of stuffed animals stampeding across the clothesline in the sun, clipped by an ear or a tail.

One evening, when I called the pupz for dinner, Bear didn't appear. He *never* missed a meal! There he was, in the backyard, sitting below the clothesline and staring longingly up at his favorite toys. I unclipped Pink Pig and he happily carried her in the house, still damp but clean, at least for a little while.

Rural living with the pupz meant taking the good with the gross: mud, ticks, burrs, and many wild, tasty critters to be hunted. Although Bear wasn't a hunter like Sammi, he occasionally found some nasty dead thing, and when he did he was so proud of himself. During one of his late fall rambles, I was out picking up sticks and tossing them into the fire pit when I saw Bear heading up Turner Trail from the cornfield with something in his mouth. I couldn't tell what it was but he carried it awkwardly. Our neighbors hunted and it was deer season, so I guessed he had some deer part—I was not wrong. As he came closer, I saw it was a freshly cut-off head, carried by the stump of the spine: *See what I caught, Mom?* He brought it right to me and I praised him for being such a masterful hunter, but with Red and Sammi out and about in the yard, I knew there'd be a big fight if they discovered it. Ever the sweet, trusting boy, Bear surrendered the head when I asked for it—thank goodness I was wearing work gloves. Now, what to do with it? Burying it meant one of the guys would just dig it up, and putting it in the trash meant it would stink, so since I had the fire going, in it went. As it sizzled and spit, Bear sat next to me, drooling. Feeling guilty for stealing his tasty treasure, I made a trip to the house and fetched him a special treat.

Gross, smelly stuff was also great to roll in and our guys, each with their own approach, turned the process into a fine art. When Sammi came upon something he deemed roll-worthy he'd stop still, nose to the ground then, as if in a trance, his whole body and head would begin to sway back and forth. If we saw him in time, "Sammi, no!" broke the spell and he'd move on to something else. If we didn't, he'd drop so fast and roll so intensely that a bath was the only option. Red gave no prior warning: he'd do a quick somersault and grind the stink into his beautiful, long coat. Bath time for him, too. Bear never rolled in stinky stuff; he just ate it. One gulp and whatever it was disappeared.

Along with the good and bad came the *really* bad, and although we'd learned to roll with the punches, Sammi caught us unprepared.

In early 2003, he began acting strangely, refusing food and not being our Silly Sammi. A scan showed a mass in his colon, and exploratory surgery confirmed the worst: colon cancer. We were beyond devastated. With all he'd been through during the myositis, it was especially cruel that he now faced cancer.

Our vet, Dr. Mooney, called us during the exploratory surgery to review our options. She could remove part of the colon and hope the cancer hadn't spread (but the risk of infection was high); euthanize him; or close him up so we could take him home to love for as long as he had left. The colon-removal surgery risks were too great, and we couldn't euthanize him—Sammi's strong spirit deserved a fighting chance—so we brought him home and nursed him as best we could, knowing each day was borrowed time. Sammi carried on for six more weeks.

When we got him home, Red and Bear immediately sensed something wasn't right, alternating between trying to get Sammi to play and staying quietly close by. But Sammi was so strong and determined—nothing kept him down for long. The morning of his third day back the pupz took a long, meandering walk together, looping through the pasture and field and back up Turner Trail. From the yard, we watched the three tails, absorbing the comfort of seeing the pack doing such a normal thing. Normal was exceptional considering the circumstances and what lay ahead. We took each moment as it came.

Feeding Sammi was very hard. At first, food wouldn't stay down, but he ate small amounts and drank water, so he wasn't giving up without a fight. The vet gave us a liquid nutrient and although Sammi was not a fan of that large syringe in his mouth, he took it like a champ and most of the time the solution stayed down.

After a while he had better luck with regular food, although there were good days and bad. Some days he was hungry, some days not, and sometimes his appetite varied hour by hour, so we tried different, creative food combinations. At a thrift store in town, Kevin spotted an old-fashioned, hand-crank meat grinder—what a great find! Cooked ground chicken became a Sammi favorite, and we rotated it with ground beef and tuna, sometimes mixing in some cornbread, which he loved. Finding new foods to tempt him was an adventure and as his needs and wants swung wildly, we followed along.

From Kevin's journal, February 22, 2003: "Every day's a good day when Sammi eats."

Sammi knew what he needed and told us what he wanted. As his energy fluctuated he began asking to go out through the front door, avoiding the steps and putting the porch ramp to good use. When he was up to it, we'd all walk Penlan Park and he'd wade through the snow, sniffing for critters in the drifts. Sitting on our favorite log, we'd watch the pupz have fun, savoring each minute. Knowing that Sammi still enjoyed life was our guidepost. Kevin and I were on an emotional roller coaster, but Sammi lived each day in the moment with no knowledge of what was to come, only what he felt in the here and now.

On his off days, he wasn't hungry and stayed inside, close to us—Kevin's studio was a favorite place and Sammi spent hours there with his dad. Kevin began a journal right after Sammi's diagnosis and, never one to share his deep feelings verbally, he poured them all out through writing. Sammi was his special boy and they shared a bond as deep as mine was with Red. There was no way to prepare for the coming loss, but writing helped frame Sammi's life, giving permanence to the joy and acknowledging the sorrow.

Sammi was our body-contact boy, and he sometimes sat, head on a lap, looking up into our eyes: *Something's very wrong inside.* Holding him close, we gave him all the energy and comfort we could, trying to conceal the ache in our hearts. Worst were the times he wanted to be alone, going into another room to lie down. He didn't seem to be in pain; it was just part of the process. Having gone through it with Müsta and Lapsi we knew the signs to watch for, even though we desperately didn't want to see them. But Sammi was such a fighter he bounced back each time, and we rode the roller coaster with him.

As the cancer disrupted his system, he continued to lose weight. He was still on the liquid nutrient but the loss of appetite was taking its toll. The down days became more frequent and some days, in his eyes, we could see the turning inward. The end was getting close.

Wednesday, February 26th, was a really bad day. Sammi took his nutrient and ate a little cornbread for breakfast, but he couldn't hold it down and his energy was very low. He wasn't drinking water on his own and the nutrient wasn't keeping him hydrated—his eyes told us he was tired. We scheduled the house call for 11:30 the next morning.

Just before midnight, we all went outside. The night was magic with soft snow all around and crisp stars in a cloudless sky. Red and Bear nosed around in the drifts, but Sammi was content to lie at our feet, breathing the winter air deeply, so aware of everything. To the eternal sky, Kevin and I spoke a whispered prayer that Sammi would, on his own, cross over from this life tonight: "Please, Sammi, go in peace—sleep away, sweet boy."

February 27th was supposed to be the day. At 11:00 a.m. we'd mix a sedative in with the nutrient to help him relax, then the vet would arrive and Sammi would leave our lives.

We got up early to get our chores out of the way, but right from the start each of us, privately, held doubts. Sammi had slept well through the night and although he didn't eat any breakfast, he was more energized than he'd been in several days, and his eyes were bright. Outside in the sun, Sammi wandered around, then went and laid under the lollipop maple, in the same spot Müsta chose on his last day. But unlike Müsta, Sammi was alert, sniffing the air and watching us as we moved around the yard with Red and Bear. He got up and walked over to Big Red, touching it gently with his nose then looking up at us: *Remember?* He laid next to the ball until we all headed into the house.

Inside, I gave them all a treat and Sammi ate a small piece and then guarded the rest of it, something he hadn't done in quite a while. As the morning went along, Sammi joined Kevin's exercise routine, then followed me upstairs while I showered and dressed—he actually had energy for the stairs! When our friend Mike arrived to say his goodbye, Sammi surprised him with happy barking and my doubts about our plans began to grow.

For our last walk together, we headed down Turner Trail. With Sammi on a leash, I stopped at the gas well while Kevin, Red, and Bear continued on toward Penlan Park, breaking a trail through the deep snow. But as they crossed the road and entered the woods, Sammi began pulling at the leash: *Let's go, Mom, what are you waiting for?!* Obviously he wanted to go along so I unclipped the leash, letting him do as he pleased.

Moving with slow determination, he followed Kevin's trail and I tagged along in case Sammi fell or needed help. Kevin, Red, and Bear turned and watched as we came toward them across the field. On the way back to the house, as the pupz roamed through the snow, Kevin and I shared our observations and misgivings; the plans for today were in motion, but maybe they were the wrong plans. Sammi wasn't withdrawn from us the way Müsta had been, and even though he hadn't eaten much in the last two days, he was energetic.

Back inside, we talked about what to do and as we sat, agonizing, Susie stopped by. Sammi shocked us all by standing up against the door to greet her with a wagging tail. Over coffee we shared our doubts with Susie, and a huge weight lifted as she agreed that today was not his time.

"Remember your guide; read his eyes and trust," Susie said, helping us step back. So immersed in the intense, daily care of Sammi, we'd forgotten that Sammi was in charge and he would tell us, in his own time and in no uncertain terms, when he was ready. I called Dr. Mooney and told her the plans had changed.

After Susie left, we all went back out in the sun. We'd been so prepared for the day to be total agony and felt whiplashed by the sudden turn of events.

"You know Sammi. We should have known he'd pull a fast one on us!" Kevin said, bringing us both a smile.

That evening, as the pupz slept around the fireplace, Sammi joined in the paw twitching and soft yips as the dream bunnies dashed away. Whatever was to come couldn't dim the incredible gift we'd been given: another day with Sammi.

The journey continued six more days, his indomitable spirit battling his fading body.

I arrived home and Sammi greeted me at the door with a stuffed toy in his mouth, the first time he'd done so in several weeks. But later he was restless and uncomfortable; a crushed Tums helped him sleep through the night. Even though his will to live was strong, he was very aware now that his system was failing, and we again saw the signs of him turning inward.

Kevin's journal entry, March 3rd: "Sammi is definitely on a journey, and he keeps journeying back to us."

On March 4th, Sammi rallied again and we all enjoyed some outside time in the evening; then Sammi walked over to the truck door. The passenger's bucket seat was a favorite spot, so Kevin lifted him up and joined him in the cab, closing the door, closing them together in their own little world.

Kevin sat in the truck with Sammi for a long time, just being with his boy, and my heart broke for him. This loss, while devastating for me, would be agony for Kevin—they were best buddies. After Sammi was gone, Kevin would be adrift.

March 5, 2003, Sammi told us. He ate nothing, refused the syringes of both nutrient and water, and our normally sweet, loving boy was grumpy and aloof. *Dad, Mom, it's time.*

At noon, he went to the door, so we all walked with him one more time around the yard. Then, back inside on the bed we'd prepared for him, I gave him the sedative. Kevin had said his goodbyes in the truck the night before, so he kissed Sammi and held him close for the last time, then went outside to be alone.

As Sammi became sleepy, I sat holding his head in my lap, gently stroking his face, so thin from the myositis and the ravages of cancer. He was ready to go.

The vet arrived, and Sammi faded from this life forever.

Why do we continue to bring dogs into our lives, and pour all our love and care into them, aware of the agony we'll endure when they pass? They strike such a balance for us, the joy of knowing them versus the pain of losing them. The joy far outweighs the loss. Grounding us in the moment, they give us a unique perspective on the passage of time. Ruled by the clock and calendar, we forget about the present and forget to acknowledge the happiness each day brings. The pupz make us remember.

Sammi had loved the pool, so with the ground frozen hard as stone, we pulled the pool from the ground and started digging his resting place in the slightly softer, low spot underneath. Red and Bear sat nearby in the snow as we dug the grave, gently nosing Sammi once in a while, saying their goodbyes. As with Müsta, we lined the grave with hay and sent Sammi on his journey with his favorite Brain Ball and tennis ball. Exhausted and completely numb, we all went inside for much-needed naps.

In the cold evening stillness, we carried on our tradition of hanging a lantern over the grave. Surrounded by moon shadows we lit the candle, hugging Red and Bear close. Our whispered, "Goodbye, Sammi," puffed in the frigid night, then disappeared.

From Kevin's journal, sometime late at night on March 5th: "Thank you, Sammi, for your love and your joy and your beautiful mind ... life has been so rich and fulfilling, living with you. When I wake up tomorrow, I won't have Sammi's eyes to clean ... who will I sing his song to? I will be lost a lot."

On the 7th, I took Red and Bear for a walk to Penlan Park and was stunned to find two pheasant feathers lying on top of the snow, at the exact spot where Sammi had stopped on his last walk. Two feathers, one for each brother. I brought them home as a reminder that Sammi was still with us.

March 9th was Kevin's birthday but our hearts were too heavy to celebrate, so our nephew Eric and his partner Becky drove from their home in Oberlin, Ohio, bringing their love and support. Eric and Becky are more like a brother and sister to us and we're united by our connection to animals. Bundled against the cold, we made a bonfire in the big fire pit, then sat and talked about Sammi, sharing our grief. After the fire mellowed down, Eric offered several cedar branches and the smoke rose in the still air, honoring Sammi's spirit.

From Kevin's journal, Monday, March 10, 2003: "We are hunkering down under a blanket of sadness."

Caring for ailing pupz demands a focus that creeps up day by day, encompassing everything, creating a kind of tunnel vision. After the intensity of caring for Sammi, our days were very empty. Together, Kevin and I had lost three pupz and while we knew what to expect and the signs to watch for, there was no way to prepare for the final, huge void. Red and Bear felt Sammi's loss keenly and our sadness, plus the upset in the routine, added to their stress. During the turmoil they'd kept us steady, following our emotions, doing their best to help us heal; seeing their worried faces now made us realize we weren't going it alone. Reassuring them helped us all.

A few weeks later, I had a wonderful dream-visit from Sammi: I was making morning smoothies and felt something press against my left leg. Looking down, there was Sammi waiting for his treat. "Sammi, you've come back!" I cried. I gave him his banana and some water, and he ate and drank. I woke up feeling him so close.

But the next several months were incredibly hard. We missed Sammi so much and talked about him constantly. Feeding the other two amplified the loss, and mornings were not the same without the prune-blop game. We listened for his nails against the floor, his Big Red brat-bark, and the squeak of his Brain Ball demanding play. We looked for him sleeping peacefully in his favorite spots around the house and yard. On our Penlan Park walks, as Red and Bear explored, we waited to see Sammi come crashing through the brush with his pack, barking with joy.

Spring came, bringing thunderstorms and memories of Sammi chasing the rumbles across the yard. Now he chased them across the sky. Run, Sammi, run!

Red became the pack leader now, but not by much. He and Bear got along so well that the change was hardly noticeable, except now they started playing together. Always in the background before, Bear became bolder, roughhousing the way Red had done with Sammi, and he began playing almost exclusively with the Brain Balls, keeping Sammi's spirit alive. Bear was still our same sweet boy, but he now stepped forward, as if he could fully be himself.

The most striking change was in Red's personality. He began to play with our cat, Mouse, who'd land soft paw punches against Red's face and race him through the house, each taking turns to let the other one win. Never one to bark much, Red became more vocal.

"Red has twice as many barks now," Kevin observed one morning.

I reminded him, "He's filling in for Sammi."

The groundhogs emerged from their winter sleep and Red surprised us by taking over Sammi's hunting role. From watching Sammi, Red knew early evening brought the groundhogs out to eat, and each day after his dinner, he stood by the back door, asking to be let out. Hiding behind the backyard flood-light pole, he'd sit perfectly still until a critter poked out of its burrow and trundled across the yard. What followed was the animal version of Red Light, Green Light. As the groundhog moved farther from its hole, Red would advance, slowly and silently lifting each foot and placing it deliberately. When the critter turned to look back,

Red froze. Gauging the distance between the hole and the animal, he moved with amazing speed at exactly the right second, grabbing the bewildered groundhog by the neck and giving a quick, lethal shake. He had his prize. Sammi never ate his kills (except for the bunnies), but Red did. Over the summer, he killed and ate six groundhogs.

The first July 4th after Sammi died felt like it had been made just for him. Thunderstorms rolled through early then cleared to make way for the fireworks. Remembering the past with his big brother, Red was excited to see the bottle rockets come out, but he didn't put the same zeal into the chase. It wasn't much fun—for any of us—without Sammi.

In a multi-pup household, there's never a good time to be unemployed, but my situation meant that I'd been able to care for Sammi throughout his cancer journey, and each day was a treasure. My freelance research clients helped carry us along financially and then, finally, after nine months, my network paid off. I landed a full-time job at an architecture and engineering firm in Columbus, building a library and doing research. It was like old-home week since many of my former design-firm colleagues worked there as well, including Sammi's former dad, Randy. I was back to the daily-commute grind, but the work was both challenging and rewarding, the company culture was fun, and my circle of critter-loving friends expanded exponentially.

Along with building my career and expanding my knowledge base, I continued to gain personal and professional confidence. Several great mentors through the years had made me realize my skills and contributions were valued and appreciated, which went a long way toward alleviating the burden of failure I still carried inside. Kevin and I also found success and satisfaction through our animal-rescue network, and through my online connections I discovered rescue transport, making trips along the Central Ohio rescue-relay to help some little waif reach its new home. It was immensely rewarding.

Bear had been with us for six happy years and while he was getting old, his exact age was a mystery. Just as trees grow bumps and lichens as they age, Bear became our Old Tree, sprouting fat tumors and warts—nothing serious, but they gave him even more character, if that was possible.

Hip arthritis bothered him, but medication brought him back to his usual, energetic self, chasing after Brain Balls and trekking with Red on Gunner rides through Penlan Park. At times, his stamina would fade before his spirit did and we'd let him set the pace, stopping to rest more frequently as the weeks went by. But he remained our sweet Sugar Bear, rambling around the yard and field, plopping himself down in the pool on hot afternoons and carrying the Frog Log off across the yard. Through it all his tail never slowed down and the happiness was clear in his eyes.

Then, toward summer's end, his health began to decline. Oh, no, not again so soon! It was obvious he'd never received proper vet care as a young pup, and he also suffered with bad grass allergies. Every summer we'd treated him with a low-dose steroid, just enough to alleviate the terrible itching. But now, his weight was slowly dropping and his liver numbers were creeping up—the steroids vs. quality-of-life balance was tilting the wrong way. We watched him carefully, as with those before.

CHAPTER 8
Play Boy: 2003

müddha

He'd known love since he was little and was a happy boy right from the start of his time with us. His soft, kind eyes were backed by a trace of stubbornness, and the Sammi boldness we knew so well.

The first Saturday in August 2003, we adopted another dog from Randy. About two years old, he was very overweight from too many table treats, but the Spa MüFarm exercise and diet would take the pounds off in a hurry. Randy's boys had named him Mikey, which we weren't crazy about, so a new name would follow in due time.

After the introductory sniff-fest was over, Kevin took Mikey and Red on a hike while I stayed behind with Bear. He was very weak—even walking around the yard was hard—and he was beginning to struggle more than was acceptable. But he was doing his best and after the recent loss of Sammi, it was nearly impossible to face the idea of losing Bear. Content to sit with me, Bear watched Mikey's introduction to the MüFarm field, and I found myself wondering what Mikey would bring to our lives. As he settled in and found his sense of place on the farm and within the pack, who would this new boy become; what wisdom would he share?

Like Bear, Mikey was a chowhound, inhaling his food then eyeing the other bowls, so dinnertime the first night was more raucous than usual. Bear's pace was slower and he laid down with his bowl in front of him, but he still managed to clean up every crumb while Mikey stood by, hoping for leftovers. Until Mikey learned his food manners we watched him—he was tempted but sat like a good boy until Bear got up and walked away. Mikey's first night with us was quiet.

After breakfast the next day, Kevin took Red and Mikey out in the morning sun. Bear lay with his untouched food in front of him, his head on his paws.

"Is my Buddy-Bear too tired this morning?" Worried, I encouraged him to eat but he turned his head away, and in his eyes was an odd, faraway look.

"It's OK, sweet boy, we'll save it for later." As I turned and set the bowl on the counter, a strange thud made me turn back.

Bear was flat out on the floor, his legs in a stiff posture, urine pooling around him; I screamed and Kevin came running. Our sweet prince lay helpless on the kitchen floor, gripped by either a stroke or seizure. Time stood still as we knelt over him. His eyes were open but fixed, his breath rapid and shallow with an occasional deep inhale. His pulse raced and his ears felt cold. Slowly, he relaxed and lay completely limp, and when I spoke his name softly, my heart broke: his perpetually wagging, happy-boy tail could not respond. Kevin called Dr. Mooney. As we waited for the vet, Bear stirred, trying to raise his head, and hope flashed through my heart. But his eyes said he was ready for his journey, even if we were not.

Bear left this life as he lived it, easily and without any resistance, happy to the very end. We doubted there would ever be another pup so filled with joy and so willing to share it with everyone.

A pair in life, it was appropriate to bury Bear right beside Sammi, next to the pup pool near the grapevine. Bear loved grapes—I'd once caught him with his head in the vines, happily munching away, and when I tapped him on the butt he turned sheepishly, his snout covered in purple. Grapes aren't good for pupz so we put up a fence to keep him out; he ate my strawberries instead.

On his soft forever bed, we curled him around his tennis ball and Brain Ball, adding his beloved Pink Pig and Penelope Pineapple.

"Sammi's waiting for you, buddy. Run now and find him."

Together they'd play with Müsta and Lapsi, the pals Bear never knew in life. Goodbye, Sugar Bear, Sweet Prince, Old Tree. Your innocent joy will overflow our hearts forever. Bear's lantern candle burned through the night as he journeyed onward.

For many years afterward, Bear's original dog-shelter newspaper photo hung, faded and curled, on the refrigerator door. His grinning pup face with the ball in his mouth made me smile every time I saw it, reminding me to always keep his happiness in my heart.

In addition to the special moments and traits we remember about our pets, there's also their simple daily presence, the space they occupy in our lives and the way they become part of everything. It's a comforting feeling and it's easy to take them for granted; they're just always there, until they're not. I remember scolding Bear once for being underfoot when I was in a hurry—we'd learned long ago never to turn around or move without looking first unless we wanted to fall on our faces. My angry voice earned me sad eyes and drooped ears, his tail suppressed but still wagging: *What, Mom? I'm sorry, Mom.* All he wanted was to be near me. He knew nothing of my hurry or why I used my harsh voice; he was just being Bear.

In that instant, I understood I needed not only to see the world through his eyes, but also to feel it through his heart. It was not up to him to understand me—I hurt my innocent, loving boy's feelings because *I* didn't understand *him!* Of course, I knew this in my head, but it took Bear's eyes to embed it in my heart. I carry the lesson with me every day. What a gift he gave me.

Over the next weeks and months, Mikey helped distract us as we dealt with our grief over both Sammi and Bear and struggled with the emptiness they left behind. Our Odd Couple, our perfect pair, was gone after so many years together; it was the end of an era on MüFarm. Red struggled as well, dealing with the double loss plus the addition of Mikey. But Red was the connection, the bridge between the old pack and the new; taking the best of his old pals, and the youth and energy of Mikey, he carried us all forward.

Even though he was young and playful, Mikey's eyes held a calmness, reflecting a deep thoughtfulness and understanding. We began calling him our Buddha-boy, which morphed into Müddha, carrying on the Müsta and MüFarm connection. It was kind of an odd name and meant nothing to anyone except us, but that was fine; it fit him well and he got used to it.

He was a handsome boy! According to Randy, his parents were both Chocolate Labs but his short, neat coat was a light yellow/gold touched with tan points, and his hair was coarse with no undercoat. His puppy picture was all Lab, but fully grown he looked more like a Rhodesian Ridgeback. He lacked the classic ridge of hair along his spine, but we saw traits in his deep, square chest; extremely muscular hindquarters; and his long, thin "pencil tail." Müddha's legs were long and slender, and when he ran flat-out he was very fast. He *loved* to swim and, was a fetching fool.

But training him was a challenge. Randy had taught him the basics but his stubborn, independent streak made teaching him good behavior somewhat difficult. Begging from the table was the hard one—apparently it had worked for him in the past—and he once grabbed food from Kevin's plate. Red was horrified: *Mom, my new brother is such a heathen!*

Through my connections we found Linda Smith, a local trainer, and we worked around Müddha's stubborn streak by keeping his mind occupied, redirecting his focus, and combining learning with play, as we'd done with Müsta. Once he learned what he could and could not get away with, everything fell into place; he became happier and a new playfulness emerged. Linda would help us with several other pupz along the way and became a lifelong friend.

Even though Müddha had never known Sammi, he almost immediately became Daddy's Boy, partially filling the huge hole Sammi had left in Kevin's life. He also became the new keeper of the Brain Balls (he preferred the large size), and as he ran toward us, shaking his head furiously, the soft rubber flopped loudly against the sides of his face. After three or four rounds of fetch, the ball would be coated with slobber and completely gross, so rather than picking it up we started Brain Ball soccer. Thrown or kicked, Müddha didn't care as long as he could fetch it.

Supervising Kevin's morning floor routine now became Müddha's responsibility, carrying on the silly exercise/playtime that had started with Müsta and continued with Sammi. Müddha was a body-contact boy, providing weight-resistance training for Kevin; when 100 pounds of Müddha leaned on him, he knew it!

But Müddha also hung out with me, especially outside. He was awed by Gunner and fascinated with all things barn-related. During barn chores, Red took up his usual spot in the doorway and relaxed, familiar with my activities, while Müddha shadowed me, curious about everything I did. With Gunner out in the pasture, Müddha watched as I puttered around, washing out the buckets and cleaning the stall, and he'd follow along as I trundled the wheelbarrow down Turner Trail to the manure pile. Even refilling Gunner's water buckets was interesting to him, and he preferred drinking from the horse buckets—especially the big trough out in the pasture—over the smaller pup-bucket. Sweeping the barn floor was my last chore and Müddha would lie down right where I needed to sweep, getting up and moving multiple times before I finished. Like Sammi, he wanted to be in on any activity.

On weekend mornings, Red always sniffed my ankles to see if I'd put on my special pants: even freshly washed, my riding jeans had the horse scent, which meant Gunner rides. Müddha learned the fun of going along, following Red through the trees, chasing and sniffing, charging ahead on the trail and circling back when I called. Müddha's extra pounds shed quickly and he matched Red's speed and agility on our long rides through the colorful woods.

Sometimes Kevin hiked with us; other times he stayed home with Müddha while Red, Gunner, and I went by ourselves, creating some of my most treasured Red memories. Following the Penlan Park trail, we'd wind our way along the path and across the creek, then beyond the normal turn-around point. Exiting the woods, we'd continue along the back of a field, then across the gravel road, before picking up a Jeep track to the trails through our neighbor's woods. Another half-mile brought us to the far corner of MüFarm.

As Gunner walked the paths I'd watch Red enjoying himself, disappearing into the fields and zig-zagging across the trails, traveling at least twice as far as Gunner and I did. Fit and strong, he could go for miles, happily sniffing and rolling in the tall grass, collecting twigs and burrs in his long coat. These were his happiest times; his place was secure, all his former mistreatment was forgotten, and we all lost ourselves in the world of those sunny fall mornings. Müddha would run to greet us as we came up through the field, and after bathing Gunner and turning him out in the pasture, I'd groom Red, brushing out bits of forest and field and watching for ticks.

In September 2003 my brother, David, and sister-in-law, Geri, who were beginning a long-term renovation on their home in Atlanta, moved into a rental that didn't allow dogs. And so cousin Pepper, a beautiful German Shorthaired Pointer, arrived for an extended visit. (She would end up staying with us for two years.) She was young and full of energy. But as a city dog she was a bit chunky—Spa MüFarm treatment for her, too!

Pepper had visited before and our pack loved her, but Red soon discovered there was competition for the groundhogs. One evening, not long after Pepper arrived on MüFarm, she suddenly took off at a dead run across the pasture. She scooted under the gate at the far end, crossed the dirt road, and ran into the soybean field—we thought she was gone for good. After much barking and thrashing around she re-emerged, trotting back toward MüFarm dragging a big, dead groundhog. Somehow, from way across the pasture, she'd scoped it out before Red. We buried it down near the edge of the field at the bottom of the Memory Garden slope. Long ago, that area had become a graveyard for wild things that had ended up dead along the roadside near MüFarm. No matter how they died, we always gave them a decent burial.

Pandemonium reigned when, a few weeks later, Beth's pup, Clyde, arrived for a one-month stay. He was a handsome red Doberman with a big, imposing presence, a (sadly) docked tail, and soft, natural ears. He, too, had visited before, but with new and different cousins, this time was a challenge. Müddha and Clyde harbored some jealousy and competition at first, but they soon discovered that playing together was much more fun than arguing. Clyde was very nimble, spinning his body around and knocking Müddha with his hip to get the play started, and then the others all joined in. Indoors or out, their young-dog energy was constant; on rainy days the house shook with their rough-and-tumble.

Red now took on the role of Official Pack Keeper. Never prone to roaming, he knew the MüFarm boundaries, and when someone transgressed, especially one of the cousins, he let us know. Red didn't stress or worry over his pack but he did police them, watching for violations and reporting back to the higher authorities. Sitting in the driveway, looking across the road and then back toward the house, his eyes told us: *You'd better come look!* Sure enough, there the two rebels were, across the road in the soybean field beyond the church: *Bad cousins!* Busted, they'd sheepishly head home, usually munching on something nasty, and be banished to MüFarm prison: the tie-out lines.

Red seemed to enjoy ratting out the criminals and we relied on him for any signs of illegal activity. The church was especially tempting. After services, several young boys would often toss a football around the churchyard and one time, Müddha couldn't resist, sneaking across the road, grabbing the football, and playing keep away. He was always ready for a game and the more the boys laughed and chased the more fun Müddha had, until we rounded him up. The caper earned him a short sentence on the tie-out line, and he learned to wait until we walked him over for playtime.

It was inevitable we'd compare Müddha to Sammi. Not that we were trying to replace Sammi—which would never happen—but there were certain things Müddha did that were so Sammi-esque. Müddha was a trash hound, getting into the wastebaskets and pulling stuff out all over the floor. And, he was even more of a body-contact boy, cramming his big-self into the smallest places to be near us: under a desk or table, or in the small downstairs bathroom. He also hated closed doors! Like Sammi, Müddha needed to know he could push the door open and be where he wanted to be. Although he didn't have Sammi's creativity, he played with the same intensity, squeezing and squeaking the Brain Ball and pushing it into the other guys, taunting them until they joined him.

Then he discovered Big Red. After Sammi died, I didn't have the heart to put the ball away and it sat, forgotten, out in the backyard until Müddha came across it one day. Curious, he nosed it, then stood pawing and barking until I went over and rolled it for him. Müddha's mouth was bigger than Sammi's, and he could pick it up and fetch it back, dropping it at our feet to demand more.

But when he learned to push Big Red himself, we put it away. Gouges in the plastic and his intense style of play bloodied his nose and bruised his front legs as he frantically pushed it across the yard. Reluctantly, I stashed the ball in the corn crib but, of course, he knew it was in there. To give him a thrill, Big Red would make an occasional appearance.

One Sammi-ism Müddha didn't share was howling. Sammi had always been a howler, triggered by coyotes in the woods or the sound of a far-off siren. Pointing his nose straight up, he'd begin a long, beautiful howl, his snout a perfect "O" as his inner wild dog took over. When Bear joined the pack we had a duet, then Red completed the trio, and whenever they stopped and tipped their heads we'd wait for the chorus. But Red didn't carry on the tradition without Sammi and Bear; all was quiet and the silence was deafening.

Sammi and Bear dream-visit, December 12, 2003:

I'm standing at the head of a line of people. I feel as though it is the type of line where you go to return something—like returning a book at the library. Although I don't turn around, I know the line behind me is long.

In front of me, a man sits in a small wooden chair. He has dark hair, but his face is nondescript; I don't recognize him. He sits casually with one leg stretched out in front of him and his arms lean on a small wooden desk. I can't see anything behind him. It's a gray mist of nothing.

At his feet lie Sammi and Bear. They see me and their tails thump the floor, but they don't get up. I see they're both in their prime. Sammi's eyes are big and round, just as they were before the myositis took over his face, and his coat is shiny and soft. His body is healthy, as it was before the cancer took him. Bear's face has the same sweet, eternal happiness it always did, and I notice the little notch in his ear flap—a souvenir from a long-ago play fight with Sammi—is not there. His body is also healthy and even though he's lying down, I know his legs are untouched by the arthritis that pained him for so long.

With tears in my eyes, I kneel to pet them and I ask, "How can they be so healthy and still be dead?" The man doesn't reply.

I stay with them for a few minutes, petting them gently and looking into their eyes. Then I know it's time to leave. As I stand, I say, "I can't leave them here," and my heart begins to ache. Even though I turn away, they make no move to follow me; they're content where they are.

I'm outside now and walking slowly down a wide set of concrete steps. There is no top or bottom to the stairs and no railing. To my left I see Sammi and Bear sitting next to the stairs and I walk over, kneel to pet them again, and whisper through tears, "Mommy will be back for you, I promise."

Then, suddenly, I'm at the bottom of the stairs and Kevin is there, as well as my dear friend Susie. I cry to them, "How can I leave them there? I have to go back for them."

They hug me and Susie says, "You can't go back for them; that's not the way it works. They had a good life."

I know she's right, and I wake up.

Not long after this dream, as if a testament to the strength of Sammi's spirit, Kevin and I began to see Sammi in the house. He'd always appear near the top of the steps in the hallway, his fluff-tail disappearing around the corner or his profile walking toward the bedroom. One night, I'd gone up to bed while the pupz were downstairs with Kevin. As I drifted off, the distinct sound of Sammi's nails jerked me awake and I jumped up, sure I'd see him. But the stairs were empty.

Clyde had returned home in mid-October, and it was odd being down to a three-pack again with Red, Müddha, and Pepper. I guess we should have known another one was waiting for us.

CHAPTER 9
Guardian-In-Chief: 2004

shaman

A pure Lab whose purpose was to look after others, he greeted us with eyes showing deep compassion mixed with anxious concern. Throughout his life he tended his pack, both critters and humans, and whenever something was not as he thought it should be, he let us know.

As Müddha's obedience lessons continued with Linda, we told her stories about our pupz, about our special love of Labrador Retrievers, and how we missed having one after losing Müsta and Bear.

"I have one you might be interested in," she said.

Shadow was a candidate at Paws With A Cause, a non-profit Linda worked for that trained assistance dogs. But Shadow's mild separation anxiety meant he wasn't suitable as a service dog and Linda was looking for a home for him. As soon as we saw him, we knew we were done for. Weighing in at nearly 100 pounds, he was a solid guy, bigger than Müsta and Bear. His coat was a beautiful cream color with soft tan frosting; toasty-colored ears framed his broad head, and his soulful, intelligent eyes missed nothing.

Shadow came home to MüFarm in March 2004, and his anxiety soon began to fade. Lots of love, exercise, and a secure sense of place were better than any calming medication. As his personality began to emerge, his whole being communicated a deep spirit and wisdom; he was an old soul. We renamed him Shaman.

The pack dynamic shifted, and we kept watch. Müddha had accepted Red as the leader, but between Red and Shaman was a subtle challenge we missed. Shaman was younger and stronger, but in his insecurity he'd attached himself to me—and no one came between Red and his mom! One day, without any obvious warning, Red jumped on Shaman, and Shaman fought back. Kevin pulled them apart and there was no bloodshed, but it frightened us—would it happen again? Fortunately, once was enough for Shaman to defer, and peace reigned afterward. But as sweet as Shaman was, he maintained a certain edge to his personality.

With the order established, Shaman and Red became buddies, tussling over toys and spending hours chasing groundhogs together. Shaman lacked Red's hunting skills and they never caught anything as a team, but they had fun trying. Like Müsta, Shaman was far too gentle to kill anything, anyway.

Shaman was so well-mannered for a one-year-old Lab; he'd learned obedience as a potential service dog, and with his compassion and desire to please, he would have made someone a fabulous assistant if not for his anxiety. And Shaman was such an easy boy. A week after we brought him home he could hike off-leash, and once he learned the Mü-Farm boundaries he never strayed—and he never let the others get away with it, either.

From the beginning, it was clear he had Müsta's compassion and Red's concern, but taken to the next level. Red had been the keeper of order, but where Red just observed and relayed, Shaman watched over everything and everyone in a worried, anxious way, reporting bad behavior and then making sure it was taken care of. If he saw something amiss, he came to find us: *Mom, you'd better come see. Dad, they're misbehaving again!* And it wasn't only the pack he worried about. Everything on MüFarm came under his watch—a baby bird fallen from a nest, or a stray dog or cat close by. Whatever it was, we had to put it right before Shaman could relax.

Shaman worked hard keeping his pack in line but he also loved to play and was a real toy boy, rooting through the plush-toy bucket and choosing his favorites from those not already claimed. At the bottom of the bucket, Shaman discovered a small lime-green and white fish with brightly striped fins and tail, and a squeaker inside. It became his favorite, and when he was tired or needed comfort, he'd pick up Green Fish and nap with it in his mouth. He also loved Bear's old stuffed soccer ball and basketball.

Of course, inside toys were different from outside toys, which created an interesting competition between Shaman and Müddha. Inside, the stuffed basketball was Shaman's, but outside, Müddha's partially deflated real basketball was his alone and, along with Brain Ball fetch, basketball soccer was a favorite game—the loud flop it made when kicked was irresistible. Then, on a field hike one day, Müddha found another old, flattened basketball; he carried it home, and soon faced a dilemma—how to guard *two* basketballs from Shaman. As big and stocky as Shaman was, he could out-maneuver Müddha, and a game of canine keep-away evolved, with Shaman teasing and Müddha chasing.

But across the years, among all the pupz, tennis balls and Brain Balls were the constant favorites—I wish I knew how many I'd bought! In the field and pasture we'd stumble upon tennis balls in all stages of decay, reminding us of Müsta's hunts behind the Antrim Park tennis courts. And frequently, while out doing yard work, I'd find old Brain Balls, forgotten under the evergreens or in the garden, the latex crumbled and rotted, the color faded. I always left them where they were.

Along with the toys and pack play, Shaman loved the outdoor life, playing in the pup pool, joining Red and Müddha on Gunner rides, or on rambles, swimming in the beans. Watching from the yard, we'd think about all the long-ago tails waving above the crops. In the beginning, it was Müsta and Sammi; then Sammi, Bear, and Red; now Red, Müddha, and Shaman (and cousin Pepper). The tails came and then left us, but the wanderings continued as one generation of the pack taught the next.

Penlan Park hikes were Shaman's favorite activity. With the freedom to run and explore, he became bolder and more self-assured. All traces of his anxiety disappeared, allowing him to discover himself, releasing the happy pup inside. But during his first summer on MüFarm, he showed us he was always on alert, a true protector, even during playtime.

After a week of late-June rain, the weather broke so Kevin and the pack headed to Penlan Park. Owl Creek was running high. An old tree, fallen across the creek, created a whirlpool; the water was sucked under the trunk and then flowed to a deep, calm swimming spot for the pupz downstream. As Kevin got comfortable on the sitting log to watch the fun, he realized Pepper was missing. Upstream, caught in the whirlpool, she was pushed up against the fallen tree and struggling against the current.

Before Kevin could make a move, Shaman streaked past him and leaped into the water. Swimming powerfully, he wedged himself between Pepper and the tree, pushing her to the creek bank and safety. Just as Müsta had saved me at Alum Creek when the sailboat capsized, Shaman was our new lifesaving-est boy.

Throughout the summer, the surprises continued. Late one evening, from way back in our neighbor's woods, came the howl of a coyote. Shaman froze, head tilted, and then from deep within, the wild, ancient sound rumbled up. Eyes closed, nose to the sky, Shaman gave his answering call; Red and Müddha joined in, and our howlers were back. Sirens set Shaman off as well, but his coyote howl had a different sound, deeper and more soulful.

And at times, we all got in on the howl-fest. On a fall road trip, as we rolled along the freeway with windows open and radio on, Kevin and I sang along to Warren Zevon's "Werewolves in London." At the "AHHH-OOOOH" chorus, the pupz all chimed in, and we laughed so hard Kevin could barely drive!

In fall 2005, with their house renovation completed, David and Geri took Pepper back home to Atlanta. She'd been part of our family for so long that it was strange not having her there—although the groundhogs probably rejoiced. Now, back to a more manageable pack of three, we expanded our weekend outings, visiting other favorite spots besides Penlan Park. Just as Sammi had always known when it was Monday night pizza pick-up time, Shaman knew when Sunday rolled around, so we combined their silliness and came up with Shammi Sunday. Each Sunday morning Shaman would remind us with bright, questioning eyes and a wagging tail that it was time for an adventure.

"Is it Shammi Sunday?" That did it! Once said, we'd better be ready to go—pupz hate the word "wait."

We'd pick a park, pack up the pack, and head out. Alum Creek was a long-time favorite spot for hiking and it got even better with the addition of a big, fully fenced dog park, including a separate fenced area with beach access. Our Shammi Sunday trips became so routine that we met the same people and dogs each week and made great new friends. Like Bear had been, Shaman was our "people dog" and became a favorite at the park.

A big, well-maintained dog park quickly becomes a very popular place, so our weekend visits started early in the day to avoid the crowds. The pupz in our regular Sunday-morning group were well-mannered, serious swimmers and fetchers, so there were several hours of peaceful fun before the rowdies arrived. It was relaxing for us before the work week and a great way to wear the guys out—which, after all, was the ultimate goal. Between the water and the sand, they got totally trashed.

Along with juggling chores, critters, remodeling, and work, Kevin and I were the children of aging parents, feeling our way along the Medicare maze, navigating the hospital-to-rehab-to-home loops, and evaluating living arrangements. Kevin lost his mom first, then his dad in 2005, about the time my parents began having trouble. Beth, David, and I cared for them between us, but I lived the closest so the heavy lifting was mine, and there were frequent (sometimes emergency) runs from MüFarm to Cleveland, 117 miles away.

Red always went along and his emotional support buoyed me through everything. Content to be with me, he was at home wherever we went, needing only a walk or two a day and sleeping quietly at the house while I shuttled Dad or Mom, or both, to and from doctors' appointments. Evenings were Red's therapy-dog time, and he'd rotate among us, resting his head on our laps. His quiet presence calmed us all.

But at home or work, my stress remained because I never knew when the next call for help would come. My small suitcase and Red's travel pack were always at the ready. Fortunately, my very supportive boss allowed me to go as needed, and Mike and Susie lifted a huge worry, jumping in with animal-sitting if Kevin and I were both away. Beth stepped in frequently, making the long drive from her home in northern Kentucky, and David and Geri sent support and advice from Atlanta, visiting when they were able.

As Dad's falls became more frequent, the search began for closer, smaller, safer living arrangements, and ended with a senior apartment in Columbus, not far from my workplace. In between, we downsized their belongings, sold their house, arranged the move, and somehow survived it all.

While I didn't miss the trips to Cleveland, I probably made twice as many shorter trips to Columbus as my parents' health slowly declined. Most of my weekday lunch hours were spent checking on them, since memory was also becoming an issue. As Kevin had experienced, I faced the odd position of being the parent to my own dad and mom, making their decisions and taking over their finances. A retired engineer, Dad's mind was always meticulous and logical, so I was shocked to discover he had three checkbook registers going at the same time, with no idea which balance was correct. I dreaded asking him about it, sure there would be strong resistance, but he handed everything over easily with a "maybe this is best" attitude; I realized his mental capacity was more limited than I'd thought.

Confiscating the car was imminent, and Dad would *not* be happy. The last time Kevin's dad ever drove, the car ended up on top of a concrete parking stop, a few feet short of a glass patio door. Luckily, no one was hurt but we couldn't take the risk again. I became the bad guy, taking Dad's keys and driving away with their freedom. Maybe to get back at me, Dad refused to use the free, convenient apartment shuttle-bus and would call me frequently for rides. The independence they'd treasured was gone forever and the pressure increased as they depended more and more on me. Dad wanted the car back, but I stood firm.

Through it all, lurking in the background, were my unvanquished feelings of failure: Am I doing the right thing? Am I being a good daughter? Should I give in on the car? I knew his body and mind were failing him, and not me, but I struggled to reconcile my feelings with what I knew was right.

Within the surrounding peace of MüFarm and reflected in the eyes of our pack, I found the support and love I needed. Through everything, Kevin was there—he knew what I was facing and gave help and advice as we navigated my parents' needs, my emotions, and the lingering self-doubt.

The senior apartment arrangement lasted only two years.

In mid-2006, Mike and Susie Baird put their house on the market and moved a few miles away, still neighbors by rural standards. Rural folk tended to stay put around us, so whenever a For Sale sign went up it was cause for much tongue-wagging as everyone speculated.

One morning, Eric, a work colleague, stopped by my desk; he and his family were looking for a rural property and someone on his team sent him to me. As we talked, we discovered they were working with our old realtor, Becky Payne, and they had just looked at Mike and Susie's house—small world!

And so before the Bairds' sale was even final, I had the inside scoop on the newcomers.

Shortly thereafter, Eric and Monica moved in with their three kids and their pup, Gracie, joining our ever-growing circle of wonderful neighbors and animal-loving critter-sitters. Over the next few years, they had one more child and acquired three horses, more dogs, and many cats. Monica turned out to be a sucker for strays, and we each took in our share.

Living rural meant many lost, lonely animals found their way to our doors, and we all became good friends with the new Morrow County dog warden, Sarina, and her staff, Crystal and Kim. Taking in strays was something we did regularly, keeping them at home if the shelter was full, and each little transient left a mark on our hearts and a memory to cherish. But that summer of 2006, a little one came along who changed our lives as much as we changed hers, and her karma rippled outward.

Hazel/Ruby — July 2006

Needing a break from the heat, I headed toward the road to retrieve the mail before going inside, but saw Shaman standing at the path leading to the front door. *Mom, something's not right!* On the porch was a small dog.

As I approached slowly she trembled, uncertainty in her eyes, but she didn't cower or run away. Talking softly to her,

I sat on the top step and she came to me tentatively, limping on her right hind leg. It didn't take long to earn her trust.

Kevin and I gave her a flea bath and dried her off, careful as we rubbed her gimpy leg and a possible rib injury on her right side. Then we introduced the rest of our pack—Shaman was particularly happy to have a new little one to look after.

Probably a Beagle/cattle dog mix, she combined the sweet Beagle face and ears with a mottled black and white cattle-dog body. She was very thin. Her nails were long so she probably hadn't walked too far, but we didn't recognize her as a neighborhood dog. She wasn't wearing a collar and when we took her to the vet, scanning revealed no microchip.

Dr. Mooney guessed her to be about a year old, gave her the needed shots, and checked her over but didn't find any broken bones; her injury would heal with time. The hunt for her owner began, but the shelter received no calls about her and there were no responses to any of my found-dog posts. Maybe she was a dump-out, or maybe she ran away and no one had bothered to look for her; we'd never know. She became part of our pack as she waited for a new home. Inspired by the humid, hazy day, we called her Hazel.

Right from the start, Hazel was a charmer. Apparently, she'd been someone's pet since she craved cuddles, and was housebroken, calm, and well-mannered. She got along famously with our pack and they loved her, sharing the beds and stuffed toys. A typical small dog, she claimed the largest bed and dragged around the biggest toys in the bucket. Careful with her injury at first, we tried to temper the play but she'd have none of it. She wasn't intimidated at all by the big boys, and was so young and full of energy that she wore our guys out.

About two weeks later, the shelter sent potential adopters to meet her. Pat and Barb visited MüFarm, fell in love with Hazel, and started the adoption process.

Pat and Barb lived in northeastern Ohio, so to save them the long drive to MüFarm we brought Hazel to a Labor Day pool party at Kevin's brother's house near Cleveland. They arrived to pick up their new family member, and what was intended to be a quick stop to get Hazel turned into an afternoon of fun and a lifelong friendship. Dog people love dog people, and Pat and Barb became extended family, attending other get-togethers and bringing their pupz, Petey, Briscoe, and Ruby (formerly Hazel).

Over the next few years, as Barb went through some personal upheavals and a divorce, her pack was always there beside her, and in fall 2012, she left her old life behind and bought a small house closer to Kevin's family. Ruby had brought us all together, but her magic wasn't finished yet. Among Barb's new friends, she met Mike on a blind date in the summer of 2013 and he joined our people/pup circle. A few years later, they moved to Florida; Mike was retiring and they were done with Ohio winters. We understood.

Across the miles, Ruby kept us connected, and when she passed away in early 2022, a part of us all went with her. Without that little stray we never would have met Barb. Our friendship would not have drawn her to move, so she probably never would have met Mike, and we would all have missed out on so much. Ruby gave us way more than we could have foreseen on that hazy July day. Given the chance, animals will change lives.

GUARDIAN-IN-CHIEF: 2004

As the years on MüFarm passed, the house and yard evolved to reflect the love, work, and money we put into the property. My family, and many of our friends, were sure we'd lost our minds when we originally bought the house—it needed *so* much work! When my dad and mom first visited, as we chattered on about our plans for the second floor, their faces clearly said: *What kind of mess has she gotten herself into now?!* All they could see were the old, cracked plaster; cobwebs; and the dirty, beaten-up floorboards. But we had a vision, and as the projects were slowly completed the successes piled up, and the old place took on a new life both inside and out.

While painting was Kevin's creative outlet, mine was gardening and the sparse but functional farmyard became my canvas. Surrounding the house, my evolving, ever-expanding perennial gardens attracted all manner of small wildlife, adding skinks, toads, snakes, praying mantises, and spring-peeper frogs to the MüFarm menagerie. Hidden among my coral bells was a large clay plant-pot tray filled with water for all the garden critters. Soft summer evenings saw swarms of bugs around our porch lights and, after a bath in the tray, toads would sit on the walkway as frogs climbed the storm door, feasting on choice moths.

Not content with the smaller, outside bathtub, the biggest of our toads regularly made his way inside the back porch through a gap under the storm door and climbed into the large ceramic water bowl. Even though it clearly said DOG in big letters on the outside, it became his private spa, forcing us to clean it each morning.

The pupz were fascinated but didn't bother the frogs and toads, and they, in return, showed no fear of the three monsters who stepped carefully around them each night. We constantly marveled at the respect the pack showed toward the tiny Mü-Farm critters. Even a praying mantis was intimidating!

Between the house, garden, and yard, the summer months were busy, but by 2007, MüFarm had settled into a good routine ... a routine about to be upended once again.

CHAPTER 10
The King of Everything: 2007

rosko

He came to us as an 18-month-old, loaded with energy, out of control, and a challenge in his *I'm so cute I can get away with anything* eyes.

In September 2007, Linda Smith contacted us about another Paws With A Cause Lab and we couldn't resist; Shaman had worked out so well, we were game for another. She warned us the new dog needed a firm but gentle hand—the understatement of the year—and we sat in her living room waiting to meet him. In he charged, up on the couch, up behind us, and down to the floor in a blur—a 100-pound, black, furry torpedo. He was beautiful.

Supposedly, he was a Golden Retriever/Labrador cross, but his short coat was a solid, shiny black and he had the square, chunky build and huge head of a Lab. The only hint of Golden we could see was the wiggle-butt when he walked. We also saw possible traces of Newfoundland in his slightly domed head; soft, soulful eyes; and heavy, squishy body. Moving with a deliberate confidence, his broad paws flipped forward with a flop as he walked, but when he wanted to, he could really run. His given name was Rhinestone, but his emerging personality was bold and a bit defiant with the deep intellect of an old soul underneath. He became Rosko, forever our big puppy.

As Shaman had, Rosko found a much-needed and consistent outlet for his abundant energy on MüFarm, helping him settle and focus. But his defiant streak challenged us; calling him earned us his *You can't make me!* look, testing us to see how much he could get away with. Little did he know we'd seen that nonsense before—there's nothing new under the sun. Following the Müsta and Müddha strategies, we combined training with play, tricking him into learning.

The pack was his best teacher. Rosko observed and quickly discovered what would earn him Shaman's worried look or Red's disapproving scowl. On field walks he'd follow the pack but then range ahead, pushing the boundaries to see how far away he could go before we called him, and even then our brat boy tested us, dawdling as if to show what a rebel he could be. When we'd turn around to head home, Rosko decided being left behind was no fun and came charging after us. Throughout his life he held onto his independence, but it was all a cover. He was kind and loyal to the bottom of his soul.

Used to having his own way, Rosko challenged Shaman at first, but a truce evolved that allowed Rosko to *think* he was king, while Shaman was the one who really kept order. Despite their initial issues they became buddies, shaking the floors and walls with their rough-and-tumble, no-holds-barred free-for-all, with Shaman giving back everything Rosko threw at him. When Müddha joined in, it was total mayhem. Size-wise, the three were an even match, body-slamming one another and bouncing right back up. Red would get in on the action, too, but Rosko was more careful with him, directing his energy upward as he jumped around, letting Red be the leader. Just as Müsta had known Lapsi was older, Rosko sensed the same in Red and toned down his rowdiness.

With four energetic, water-loving pupz, trips to the dog park were now a handful, but once at the beach they all made a beeline for the water. Like Shaman and Müddha, Rosko was an incredibly strong swimmer and they never tired out, three Labs in their glory. Tossing multiple tennis balls kept Kevin and me busy, but usually other park-goers played along, and if kids were involved, so much the better. Rosko was such a ham and kids loved him, probably because he was a total attention hog and acted like a child himself, barking and rolling on the sand, coating himself from nose to tail.

Red balanced his swimming with resting, sitting next to me on the beach. My heart-and-soul boy was about nine then; the gray was creeping across his face and his left eye showed the beginnings of a cataract. Moments of panic gripped me as I clearly saw time advancing, but I'd learned the lesson from those before: Live now, and love 'em while you've got 'em.

Healthwise, we'd seen a lot over our pup years, but lens luxation was a new one. By March 2008, Red's cataract had progressed, then overnight the eye went completely white and he began rubbing it—the lens had broken loose, blinding the eye and causing painful pressure, so Dr. Mooney recommended removing it. After all Red had been through early on, it hurt my heart to think of him being half-blind, living out his days with an empty, stitched-up eye socket, but we did what we needed to do.

After the procedure, the brothers each gave Red a thorough sniff, checking out the cone and the side of his face, and then Dr. Shaman took over, supervising Red's recovery. Red bounced back and the cone came off, but we were on watch since the condition can affect both eyes. Caught in time, surgery would save the other eye, so checking it daily became part of our routine.

Cruising through the summer of 2008, we enjoyed the relative calm and stability. The previous winter had been constant upheaval between Rosko's training, Red's eye issues, and a steep decline in my dad's health. After a bad fall, hospitalization, and rehabilitation, Dad and Mom's independent-living days were over, and in just a few weeks, we had to find a new place for them, pack up the apartment, and get them resettled.

"You've carried the load so far; now it's my turn," Beth said, as she researched places in Cincinnati so they could live closer to her. Soon we were in the throes of moving them yet again.

This would be their last move. Although Mom was more independent than Dad they both needed assisted living, but a few days after the move, Dad took another bad fall and had to go into skilled care; my stress level went through the roof. He had *hated* the rehab facility, and skilled care was no different. Being dependent on others for everything went completely against his being (which is why neither of them had wanted to live with David, Beth, or me).

Determined to have some control, Dad the engineer figured out how to disable his bed alarm and escape his room, which gave the staff fits. David, Beth, and I were not at all surprised. We were secretly proud of him for taking what little control he could get, but also pained since his frail body and confused mind no longer allowed him to have what he wanted. His independence was completely gone and although he put on a stoic face, he was miserable inside. Mom continued to live in the assisted-living apartment two floors below Dad. They hadn't lived apart in 63 years and although Mom stayed upstairs with Dad all day, every day, it wasn't the same and she worried over him.

"When can we bring Daddy home?" she kept asking. Not being able to take care of him herself anymore was hard to accept.

It was strange for me at first, not having them close by, not being the first line of defense. Beth now took the calls and made the dashes to the hospital, but with my power of attorney, I stayed very involved. Red continued to make visits with me and if Kevin came along, so did Rosko, Müddha, or Shaman, lighting up faces as we visited Dad and Mom and walked the halls and common areas.

My stress leveled somewhat but was still pervasive, and the pupz were on top of it, urging me to play, hike, or relax with a head or paw on my lap. That always fixed everything.

Right before my birthday in mid-September 2008, I lost my job at the architecture firm as the stock market stumbled, then crashed. I was stunned. Many of my friends and colleagues were in the same boat as the corporate world went into suspended animation—no one was hiring. By this point I was accustomed to setbacks, no longer taking them as personal failures, but this one was especially hard. I'd grown and developed my skills entirely in the corporate setting and that door was currently slammed shut. I couldn't see a way forward. My separation package included a free career-path counseling program and with nothing to lose, I signed up. It proved invaluable, helping me focus on the basics—what I was really good at—and envision creative ways to adapt.

Although I didn't see it at the time, the strengths I'd admired so much in Lapsi and Red throughout their lives were the same ones I called upon in those months of job searching: work around roadblocks and move forward with determination. I reconnected with some former freelance-research clients and Kevin and I instituted a spending freeze on MüFarm—please, no vet emergencies! During the difficulties, our pack came through, keeping us distracted from the troubles and focused on what really mattered.

To say Rosko was happy is an understatement. With acres to roam, tons of toys, and three brothers to play with, he was living the good life and soon became a neighborhood favorite. Whenever anyone stopped by it was a big brouhaha with all the pupz competing, each with his own attention-getting strategy. Müddha would push his Brain Ball into any empty hand, Shaman would worm his way in and lean against legs, and Red would simply stand quietly, wearing his best *please notice me* look. But Rosko would shove his big, wiggly body into the fray, flop down, roll over, and dare the visitor to ignore him, which was impossible.

Like a headstrong child, he was fearless, with a will of his own that kept us on our toes and sometimes scared us to death. Heading home one hot afternoon, we stopped at a small park along the Kokosing River to let them all cool off. With Müddha, Shaman, and Red on leashes, Rosko followed along, but we saw that the river was running way too fast for swimming. Heading back toward the car, we realized Rosko wasn't behind us—then we saw him in the water. He was a very strong swimmer but the current was sweeping him downstream. While I held the other three, Kevin raced frantically along the bank, screaming for Rosko, but he lost sight of him. Kevin turned back with panic on his face. Then, out of the brush along the riverbank came a soaking-wet Rosko, strolling toward us at his typical leisurely pace. *What's all the fuss about?* Our relief was huge!

Even on MüFarm we kept an eye on him. A few weeks after the river episode, a neighbor from up the road pulled in the driveway and rolled down her window. There was Rosko in the back seat, sitting happily between her two young children. The neighbor laughed and opened the back door, but Rosko sat where he was—the kids were feeding him bits of their cookies. I bribed him with further treats and he finally climbed out, then did his best tummy-up Rosko Flop: *You can't scold such a cute puppy!* Evidently, he'd perfected his stealth-escape technique, since neither Shaman nor Red had alerted us. He was busted on the tie-out line for several days.

Lesson learned, he stayed on MüFarm after that, exploring and finding new things to get into. Like Bear, Rosko was a total food hound and inside or out, he ate anything edible (or not-so-edible) he could find. It wasn't long before he discovered the apple trees in the Memory Garden. All the guys loved fruit, and once Rosko realized there was a never-ending supply of fall apples, he ate several every day, seeds, stems, and all. When the apples turned brown and mushy, the yellow jackets would bore holes in the soft skin, but if he ever got stung it didn't bother him. Usually, he laid under the trees, eating the apples he could reach without getting up; other times he'd bring one to the yard, munching away in the evening sun—our big black bear enjoying his daily fruit. The mulberry trees out in the pasture were another favorite, and he'd eat berries until his backyard piles turned purple and were laced with tiny seeds.

Even in the house he found ways to amuse us, inserting his antics into everything. All the other pupz hated the vacuum cleaner and stayed well away, but Rosko would follow along as I moved from room to room, plopping his big-self down in front of me, demanding to be vacuumed.

"Vacuum the Rosko! Gotta get that leg ... gotta get that shoulder ... don't forget that head!" I'd sing as I passed the nozzle gently over him, waiting for him to roll over so I could do his other side. It was intensely silly and added to his already immense charm, plus it made my least-favorite household chore semi-enjoyable. He was such a character, always doing as he pleased!

As Red aged he clung more closely, following me everywhere. He loved helping me in the garden since I was down at his level, and as I'd crawl slowly around the beds he was never far away, sleeping in the soft grass or sniffing around the yard, then wandering back. Touching my ear with his nose meant *Mom, it's break time,* and then he'd sit, leaning against me as I hugged him close, my arm around his bright auburn coat, warmed by the sun. It was such a small thing, a brief moment in time, but it's a memory I hold onto.

Müddha was still my barn boy, helping with evening activities while Red snoozed and the other two hung out in the orchard. Of the four, Müddha was the outsider, preferring his people over pack activities, rambling around on his own or playing ball. Brain Ball fetch was his purpose in life, his focus and intensity surpassing even Sammi's, and the games only ended when we picked the ball up and called it quits. So when he started slowing down in late fall 2008, we worried.

Red was already on medication for arthritis, but we started seeing some stiffness in Müddha, as well, and he began having trouble with the steps. The year before, arthritis had forced the amputation of one front toe, but he'd been fine since. This new stiffness was alarming since it affected his whole body. As with Sammi's cancer diagnosis, we were caught totally by surprise when x-rays revealed the beginning of arthritis in Müddha's spine—we again faced an uphill, no-win battle. As his spine deteriorated, his pain level and mobility issues would increase. The best we could hope for was good pain management and slow progression. With supplements and meds, he returned to almost normal activity, but as fall progressed he spent more time lying down, watching the goings-on around him.

In mid-December 2008, while I was still unemployed, we faced the vet emergency we'd feared. A cataract appeared in Red's remaining eye and Dr. Mooney referred us to a canine ophthalmologist in Columbus. The eye-saving procedure was expensive, but I couldn't let my Red go totally blind. Several days and $2,000 later, we brought him home: the surgery was successful. Eventually, the cone came off and Red adjusted, carrying on as if nothing had happened. Life had dealt him so much already, this was just one more thing. His strength and adaptability inspire me to this day.

Over the winter Red's arthritis became more apparent, but Müddha was in far worse shape. An old chair in Kevin's studio became Müddha's comfort place, and except for mealtimes he spent many indoor hours curled up. Stairs were out of the question, so most nights Kevin slept on the studio couch, as he had all through Sammi's cancer battle, bringing home the reality that we might soon lose Müddha.

Shaman was very aware things were not as they should be on MüFarm, and although he worried about his two brothers he still played with Rosko, keeping him occupied and balancing our stress. Looking after us all was Shaman's mission and he took it seriously, so we did our best to stay as normal as possible. Snowy evening field walks provided Shaman with a well-earned break from the daily cares, and he'd run with Rosko in huge, sweeping circles as dusk settled down.

Sammi and Bear had once been our Odd Couple, but now Shaman and Rosko filled those roles. They were buddies, both in their prime, strong, healthy, and happy—but the similarities ended there. Shaman was the parent, fun-loving but mature and focused on those around him, open to a good time but never cutting loose completely. Rosko, on the other hand, was the class clown, the study-hall cut-up, always demanding (and usually getting) all the attention. But from under this veneer, through his eyes and straight from his heart, came a deep calm and wisdom, and even people meeting him for the first time realized there was something very special about him.

Rosko assumed Müddha's role as Daddy's Boy and exercise coach, plopping his big head on Kevin's chest and legs for weight-resistance training. Rosko's head was unlike any other pup's: heavy, but with the same soft squishiness as his body, and ears like ham slabs. Kevin and I had seen an episode of PBS' "Nature" about a species of duck called Bufflehead, and it became a Rosko nickname. When Rosko wanted attention, his big bufflehead would push open doors or land in a lap, toy in mouth, eyeing us with the same *I'm so cute* ploy he'd used the first time we saw him. A perpetual five-year-old child, he needed constant activity and was always ready for play.

At first, he didn't have a particular favorite plush toy, so he'd steal whatever toy Shaman wanted just to rile things up. But when I brought home Buzzy Bee, Rosko claimed it for his own. About the size of a softball, the bright-yellow bee had black stripes, felt feelers, and little silver wings. Best of all, when squeezed just right, it emitted a little buzzy song, sending Rosko into a silly, wiggly frenzy, rolling on his back with the toy in his mouth and then tossing it up to pounce when it landed.

Müddha continued to guide our activities and we made adjustments, letting him do as much as he could for as long as he could. While his heart and spirit remained true and strong, his body was slowly turning against him. His shoulders and hindquarters, once hard with muscles, were withered but he limped along, trying to keep up with the pack. On a mid-February 2009 walk, I stood with him in the chilly rain where Turner Trail gave way to the open field—as far as his legs would let him go. With the winter crop stubble rattling in the wind, the pack went on with Kevin toward the road and Müddha's eyes followed them, his soft whines puffing white in the cold afternoon. He wanted so much to be with them. I held the big umbrella over us both and he sat on the damp ground until the pain made him rise, then we turned to make our way back toward the house, stopping frequently to rest. He panted, even in the cold—it would be time to switch pain medications soon.

THE KING OF EVERYTHING: 2007

In spite of it all, his Brain Ball addiction continued, and to keep him in on the play activities we got creative: we'd kick the ball, he'd catch it, and then we'd fetch it from him. As long as he could still stand it was game on, and even lying down he'd bark for more ball play. The house and yard were his world now and one of us stayed with him while the others went off across the field. Sitting with him brought back the times we'd done the same with Sammi and Bear, feeling the helpless acceptance. Little did we know the heartache that lay ahead.

Amid all the pack chaos, I started a new job on April 1st and was getting used to new colleagues in a totally different field. Confident in my research skills, I landed in the development office at a nearby college, providing background information on potential donors. It was interesting researching people instead of industry-related topics, and while the office atmosphere and benefits were great, the pay was well below corporate standards, so I kept my ear to the ground.

Barely two weeks later, my dad's health failed and I made multiple runs to Cincinnati. The Atlanta family joined us, and on April 11th, Dad passed away. Now in uncharted waters, we helped Mom along while dealing with our own grief. I'd always been closer to my mom, so watching her come to terms with her loss was difficult; her life revolved around her husband and children, and now she was on her own. But, always unflappable, she slowly adjusted—I guess after raising four kids through the '60s and '70s, she could handle anything. Her assisted-living apartment was safe and secure, providing the daily help she needed, and although she missed Dad, she never complained. On our calls and visits, her warm, loving smile was there for us, as always.

And I had my own issues. It had been hard being my dad's daughter, growing up under a cloud of failed expectations, always trying to prove myself but coming up short. I understood he loved me, but I resented the pressure he put on me. All through school I'd had no desire or ability to absorb what I was supposed to be learning and I struggled with most subjects, especially math. For an engineer, that must have been impossible to understand.

From flashcards and Mom's patient guidance, we kids learned our math basics—partly because Sue or I would hold up fingers behind Mom's back to give each other the answers. But when I got to geometry and algebra, Dad took over the homework help, and I froze. I wanted to understand but I just didn't get it, and his disappointment was palpable. One evening, I was so lost and nervous I couldn't pay attention, and my fingers fiddled with a little plastic tape dispenser. Dad grabbed it and threw it across the room in frustration. In that moment, I gave up. I was a failure and would never please him, so I stopped trying. Even my small successes earned me the response: "Next time you'll do better." I suppose the goal was to make me try harder, but it only confirmed that nothing I did was ever good enough. I learned to be hard on myself, as well, with a "do it right or don't do it" attitude and an inability to forgive myself when something did go wrong.

As a former elementary school teacher, Mom understood that children learned what they lived, and every word and action was a lesson. She told me once that the hardest part about being a parent was always needing to set a good example, because she never knew what her kids would remember. I never forgot Dad's tape episode, and it shaped and defined me for most of my life.

Growing up behind my brother, David, was also a challenge—I was in awe of him. Extremely talented artistically, he always seemed to know what he would become, and even though I'm sure he faced doubts and struggles, he was a hard act to follow. I loved and admired him, and from my younger perspective, his successes in college, career, and marriage set a precedent I couldn't hope to follow.

The irony of it all was that once I finally got to college, I ended up with nearly straight A's and even tutored other students in math. One thing Dad had given me was a logical, mechanical mind, a straightforward ability to think through a problem and efficiently get from point A to point B. Out on my own, away from Dad's pressure to succeed, everything clicked.

After my college and career successes, I think I assumed that my feelings of failure would disappear. They didn't, and even after Dad passed away, the resentment and need to prove myself tumbled through my life. Looking back now, I realize Dad faced his own struggles and pressures, and when his hopes for me didn't materialize I became one more worry. I understand it. But it doesn't make me feel much better.

Spring came and Müddha's eyes began to show a puzzlement, as if he couldn't understand why his body would no longer do what he wanted. Joining us outside in the sun, he'd make his way stiffly down the ramp, lying in the yard as the play went on around him. Walking was about all he could do, moving slowly along, doing his outside duties, nosing his toys and barking. The will to play was still so strong, but after a few Brain Ball kicks he'd begin to stumble. It was heartbreaking, but the pain meds kept him comfortable, and he carried on.

One afternoon in late-April, Red was with me in the south garden while the other pupz played in the backyard. As Kevin turned his car into the drive, Rosko came charging from behind the house and, instead of going around Red, he barreled into him, hitting him on his blind side and knocking him over. Red gave a loud, surprised yip—I ran to him immediately. He was dazed but shook it off, then joined in the happy barking as Kevin parked by the barn. I couldn't be angry with Rosko, but I felt terrible Red hadn't seen Rosko coming and had no chance to get out of the way.

A few days later, Red started having trouble. He was on and off his food and had bouts of vomiting and diarrhea; bloodwork showed extremely high liver numbers.

"Prepare yourself. This is bad," Dr. Mooney told us. She knew how much Red meant to me, and Red also held a special place in her heart.

I was in shock. Numb with fear, my mind was in turmoil. Had he eaten something toxic? We didn't keep any poisons, and cleaning products were well out of reach. Did he have some kind of infection? Nothing showed up in any of the tests. It wasn't until well afterward that I made the connection between Rosko knocking Red down and the liver problem, and by then it was far too late.

THE KING OF EVERYTHING: 2007

The next week was a blur. Red deteriorated so fast and I tried in vain to face what was coming. He was unable to hold down any food and barely any water; his diarrhea was getting worse and he was rapidly losing weight. Totally helpless, I sat on the floor with him in the evenings, trying to find some peace, and sometimes Müddha laid down with us, sharing the connection and comfort. Seeing one of our guys decline was bad enough, but two was devastating and I moved through the days in a trance.

Then, the day came when I saw in Red's eyes the eternal love and trust—but I also saw pain and the subtle but unmistakable request. I knew what he was asking.

April 29, 2009. I spent the night on the couch; Red was on his bed next to me, weary and dehydrated. My hand rested on his shoulder, connected to him.

"Because I love you, I'll do this. For you. Because you accept it, I will have to. Please show me how." I don't remember anything else except the feel of his warm coat under my hand. Somehow, I slept.

In the morning, we got Red up and outside. He headed toward the barn but could only make it partway. To help Müddha get around, Kevin had rigged up his dad's old wheelchair with a padded plywood platform to make the seat area bigger; we lifted Red onto the chair and wheeled him into the barn to wait for the vet. Red's favorite place to be was lying in the barn door, sleeping with the sun on his face while Mom did chores. It was right we should be there together at the end.

Gunner was already out in the pasture for the day, so all was quiet; overhead, barn swallows swooped and dived on whisper wings. Red lay still as I knelt in front of him, holding his head in my hands. Too dazed to cry, I tried to conceal my pain, but my heart was his and I couldn't hide anything from him. Leaning close, I whispered, "Please wait for me, and come back to me somehow, if you can. I'll always be here, waiting for you."

Dr. Mooney had given up her large-animal practice but made a special barn call for Red. She hugged me with tears in her eyes, then eased Red from the here and now, leaving us to grieve wildly. I sat for a long time, not thinking or feeling anything, completely blank inside. My heart would never be the same. A chunk of my soul was gone.

Joining the line of graves by the corn crib, we buried Red next to Sammi and Bear, with shreds of his favorite Green Gator snugged under his head. At dusk, we stood with our pack and lit his passage candle lantern, and that was the beginning of the unimaginable: our lives without him.

Journey on, my sweet Red. You were so loving, giving everything you had; so brave, trusting your heart to me after such terrible neglect; so accepting of everything. There will never be another one like you.

Failure compounded my hideous grief and I beat myself up relentlessly, questioning myself on so many levels. If I was so observant and in tune with my pupz, how could I have missed the connection between the blow Red took and his liver failure? I hadn't even thought of it so didn't mention it to Dr. Mooney. If I was such a good researcher, why hadn't I discovered the possibility of a bruised liver? Would it have made any difference? How could I have let my soulmate down in the worst way? If I'd done my best, maybe something could have been done for him, maybe my boy would still be with me. When he'd needed me the most, I'd failed him; there was no denying it. It haunted me for a long time.

I told myself how worried Red would be if he saw my sadness, how he'd come and lean against me, trying to make me feel better. Wishing for the time back, all I could do was keep him in my heart and try to move forward.

I was humbled and heartbroken.

Sometimes with multiple pupz, the grief comes in waves, and now we were facing the imminent loss of Müddha. By mid-May, his spinal arthritis was so bad he could no longer walk and needed the wheelchair full-time to go up and down the ramp. Inside, he spent all his time curled up in his chair, which was no way for him to live—but the problem was, he wasn't ready to go. His appetite was fine, his eyes were still bright and curious, and pain medication kept him comfortable. But what do you do with a 100-pound pup who can't walk or even stand on his own? He couldn't play, he couldn't go on hikes, and when we took him outside on the wheelchair, he'd see Rosko and Shaman roughhousing and struggle to get up. But even with both of us holding him, he could no longer support himself. Müddha was the first of our pupz who wasn't ready when we had to make the decision.

Dr. Mooney made another house call. On the south porch in the morning sun, he faded from our lives, and we were struck again by the wonder, the joy, and the pain of loving them. Every loss brings memories, marking the passing of their years—but what about the years Müddha should have had, happily playing Brain Ball and going on hikes? This loss was so bitter, his life cut short—he was only 8 years old.

Outside, his favorite place to lie down had been the Müddha Hill, a gentle rise at the sunny southwest corner of the barn, in sight of the house and yard. It would be his forever spot. But digging the grave was a challenge, as if Müddha was still telling us he wasn't ready to go. The land near the south field had always been rocky. Each time Kevin stuck the shovel in he'd hit a rock, and some of them were large, requiring a ratchet strap and pulley to wrench them from the ground. But it was Müddha's special place; it was where he belonged.

Finally, by late afternoon we had a perfect grave, a pile of rocks, and not much soil for fill-in. Still numb from Red's passing, we laid to rest our Müddha Buddha boy on a bed of hay with his beloved Brain Ball. After he'd shown such bravery in the face of pain, and determination against adversity, we had to be strong; Müddha would expect nothing less. Shouldering the loss and setting our weariness aside, we dug soil from the edge of the field and filled in the grave, using one of the boulders for his headstone. By the time we finished, it was dark. Lighting his lantern, we stood in shared disbelief—another of our pupz was gone. Rosko and Shaman had to say goodbye again, way too soon.

But 2009 wasn't finished with us yet. Only a few weeks after we buried Müddha, Gunner began favoring his right-front hoof and Dr. Krueger, my new horse vet, found an abscessed stone bruise. With treatment, the abscess finally broke out at the top of the hoof, but by then Gunner had developed laminitis in his left-front hoof from bearing the extra weight. Once again, we faced a serious battle.

THE KING OF EVERYTHING: 2007

Gunner was a beautiful boy. A pampered show horse since he was a weanling, he'd grown up in the cycle of training, grooming, trailering, and performing, with a little leisure time in between. But he was tougher than he looked. We were a team and I promised him I'd be there and do everything I could—I would *not* lose him, too. For hours each day, Gunner stood patiently while I ran cold water over the inflamed hoof, gave him his medicine, and cut pieces of foam insulation board, taping them to the bottom of his hooves to help relieve the pressure. On workdays, Susie took over the treatment, caring for Gunner as if he were one of her own. We battled together for three weeks, but in the end it wasn't enough. On July 12th, the vet came and we lost another one. It was nearly unbearable.

Neighbors help neighbors. The backhoe came and we buried Gunner next to Missy under the horse chestnut tree.

That evening, I spent time alone in the barn with Rosko and Shaman, putting things away, sweeping the floor, cleaning the stall one last time. Where was Müddha, my barn helper, and Red, lying in the doorway? Gunner should be there, happily eating his dinner and munching his hay—his huge presence was suddenly gone. As I shut the stall gate, the clang of metal against wood echoed in the emptiness. With Shaman and Rosko at my feet, I leaned my head on the gate and everything poured out in exhausted, exquisite grief. Too wrung out to even stand, I sat on the floor and held them close. Our little farm was *so* lonely.

Familiar now with the waves of grief, they rolled over Kevin and me at will, carrying us along, wearing us out, and depositing us back on the rock of MüFarm. Such quick, dramatic shifts, so close together, knocked our whole world off-kilter. Rosko and Shaman were at a loss, too, and we all closed in around one another, hunkering down under our blanket of sadness. Our Shammi Sunday dog park trips forced us to maintain some normalcy and our friends were very supportive—it was good to spend time among those who knew what we were going through.

But at times the emptiness was so overwhelming, all we could do was hold tight to the memories. Each morning and evening, two now-unused food bowls sat in the kitchen, but putting them away was harder than seeing them empty and forlorn. And half of our daily routine was also missing. When we headed out the back door in the morning, there was no whinny to greet us, demanding breakfast. As the pupz did their duties, I was at a loss, not even able to go near the barn. For several weeks, the barn doors remained closed; the empty stall and emotional void were too big to face. Returning from our evening field walks, I'd catch myself scanning the pasture while Rosko and Shaman ducked under the gate, looking for Gunner. Wandering up Turner Trail, they'd head toward the barn: *Mom, it's stall-cleaning time, remember?* Each day was a struggle, but gradually we moved forward, coaxed along by Rosko's demands for play and the worry plainly written on Shaman's face.

Then fall came, and brought along a little one who needed us as much as we needed him.

CHAPTER 11

Light in the Darkness: 2009

shadow

The dog shelter announcements in our little county newspaper got me again: near the last page was a picture that went to my heart. There was something about his eyes and the confused, forlorn look on his face—I stared at the photo for several long minutes and couldn't turn the page. I knew there was room again for one more.

I left the newspaper on the table and went about the rest of my day. When Kevin got home it still lay open in the dining room.

"He looks so broken." Kevin said, putting into words what had struck me about Shadow's expression.

The description under the photo told us Shadow was old—the family who'd surrendered him said he was 12, but he looked older. At the shelter, Crystal brought him from the kennel and we were surprised by how little he was; at about 30 pounds, he'd be our smallest one yet. He walked stiffly, looking up with cloudy eyes, and we noticed he was missing a few front teeth. Under his filthy, matted coat, his weight was good—his elderly owner, unable to groom or bathe him, had at least fed him well. Whatever time remained for Shadow, we decided, would not be spent in the shelter.

Home he came and went right into the laundry tub. After several soapings and rinses most of the mats came out, and from under all the dirt emerged the black coat and white chest bib of an Australian Shepherd, four white feet with black freckles, and a tiny white tip at the end of his fluffy tail. A trip to the vet confirmed arthritis, cataracts, hearing loss, and congestive heart failure, but he was a happy little guy, always wagging his tail and hoping for a treat.

Apparently, Shadow had lived outside, but old dogs can learn new tricks. In no time he was housebroken, sharing the prime sleeping spots, displaying his begging talents in the kitchen, and playing with his new brothers. Rosko was especially fond of him and toned down his play, but Shadow showed incredible energy, jumping on Rosko, who'd tumble over, pretending Shadow had knocked him down. Feet flailed amid much play snarling and barking, with Rosko writhing on his back, feet kicking and launching Shadow backward. But Shadow would always charge back to jump on Rosko again.

Shaman also romped with Shadow, doing his best play bow and bringing toys into the fracas. It was hard to believe Shadow was 12-plus years old, and incredible that such an old, frail little dog could act more like a puppy than either of his much younger, much larger brothers. Whatever they threw at him, he gave it right back, and the house and yard were once again alive with silliness and laughter.

As I watched them, my heart ached thinking of Müddha's Brain Ball fetch, and of Red playing with all his brothers: from Sammi to Rosko, Red was the link across the pup years. I missed Red and Müddha so much, and I found myself thinking my shadows would be right there every time I turned around. Without Gunner, there were no Penlan Park rides through the colorful crunchiness—no Red running on ahead, his auburn coat blending with the fall leaves, no Müddha charging across the field to greet us. The memories made the days a little easier, and we leaned on our love of Shaman, Rosko, and our new little Shadow.

After Dad passed away, Beth and I visited Mom often. Mom missed Dad terribly, and most days she'd take the elevator up to his old floor to sit in the common area and chat with some of the residents. More gregarious than Dad, she made a few friends, but mostly she read the paper or watched the always-on TV.

Shadow took on Red's former role as my sidekick and helper on these visits, and everyone loved him. Happy and outgoing, he charmed the staff and residents, turning my visits into all-day affairs as we made our way along the halls, stopping for all the attention. Mom made a big fuss over him, greeting him as if every time was the first time.

"He's so sweet! Where did you get him?"

"Oh, I love those little white feet!"

"He's so small! How much does he weigh?"

"He's such a lucky little dog."

The conversation was the same each visit as I told her all about him.

Mom had broken her hip in mid-2009 and after she recovered, she gave up her little apartment and moved to skilled-nursing care. I think she was actually happier. There was much more activity, more interaction with the staff, and her new neighbor became a friend. On my visits I'd find them on the couch together, engrossed in a long, rambling conversation that made sense only to the two of them, but it was wonderful to see them smiling and laughing. Shadow would become their center of attention for a while before they'd go back to their chat, and then Shadow and I would make our rounds.

Sensing which residents needed the most attention, Shadow brought smiles to lonely faces and prompted shaky hands to reach out. His favorite resident (besides Mom) always sat outside her room in her wheelchair, alone. Nearly catatonic, she didn't lift her head, speak, or move. But when Shadow approached, her hand would come forward very slowly; her pale fingers would gently touch his soft fur as he stood up and put his head in her lap.

Then, one day, she wasn't there. Puzzled, Shadow stood in front of her room, then poked his head inside the door. But she was gone. The nurse told me Shadow's visits were the only time the old woman had ever moved.

With the weather turning chilly, I made Shadow a fleece-lined denim coat with a wide belly-band to keep his tummy warm, and we passed the winter walking the snowy Penlan Park trails. He was a trooper, keeping up with the big boys, rooting through the drifts; his jacket always came home covered in snow.

On an early spring hike in 2010, we noticed Shadow was missing so I started walking back along the trail, since I knew he wouldn't hear me calling. A low growling sound drew me and I found him with his head buried in a huge pile of brush, pulling and jerking on something. He was seriously into whatever he was after so I stood and watched; to my total amazement, he pulled out an opossum nearly his size! Tugging and shaking, he was working so hard at it I didn't have the heart to intervene. I doubted he could really harm the critter, anyway.

I could hear Kevin and the other pupz backtracking as well, so to head off a big fight over the prize, I clipped on Shadow's leash and tugged him gently away. After a while the possum uncurled, blinked, and looked around as if trying to figure out what happened, then trundled back into the pile. Shadow lost his orange bandana in the melee, buried deep inside the sticks, so we left it there and went on with our hike. It's probably still there to this day.

On a Sunday in early June, a bad cold knocked me flat and I spent most of the day on the couch. The pack napped nearby and although Shadow was breathing faster than normal, he didn't appear to be in distress. That night, he slept with us as usual. In the morning, after Kevin left, I rested on the couch but Shaman came to me with his worried look: *Something's not right.* Shadow was panting. The vet couldn't see him until after lunch, but within half an hour it was clear something was seriously wrong. The panting was worse and Shadow was very restless, pacing back and forth between me and the door. I called the vet to report the emergency, then put him on the back-door tie-out while I ran to get dressed.

But it was too late. I found him lying in my flower garden, breathing heavily. I dropped to my knees and his eyes opened halfway; he was already turning inward. Determined that his last minutes wouldn't be spent in a mad, futile rush to the vet, I stroked him gently as my tears fell on his sun-warmed coat. He inhaled, then coughed up a large amount of clear fluid with his last breath as his little heart failed. Shadow died curled in my arms, surrounded by love, as Rosko and Shaman sat with me, saying their goodbyes.

Kevin came home and we dug yet another grave, out near the corn crib next to Sammi, Bear, and Red. Shaman and Rosko stood with us as we lit the lantern candle, and we wondered aloud how Shadow's little soul could have made such an impact. He was with us only eight months, but the tears were hard and the loss huge. The life of the party every day, he'd brought MüFarm so much joy after a time of terrible sadness and loss. Plucked from a lonely end at the shelter, he taught us happiness in the face of overwhelming grief; fate brought us together at exactly the right time.

We had a friend years ago who could never bring herself to get another dog after her old one died. She couldn't bear the heartbreak again, couldn't imagine trying to replace her beloved companion. It hurt us to think that someone with so much love for dogs couldn't open her heart and share it again. For us, *not* having another dog would be unbearable. Seven times we'd been through the pain and knew those lost could never be replaced. But the new ones have so much magic, revealing themselves slowly, tricking our hearts into loving them even though we know that they, too, will become irreplaceable. Because they are each their own, they'll leave their special mark on our hearts, as treasured as all those gone before.

And that's what keeps us coming back for more! Discovering each of them is so much fun, we don't ever want it to end.

CHAPTER 12
Home at Last: 2010

boobear

After being returned to the Morrow County Dog Shelter twice before age two, his eyes wore a defeated, uncertain look. But still visible was a tiny spark of hope—he simply wanted a chance, and a place to belong.

The MüFarm two-pack didn't last long. A few weeks after Shadow left us we headed back to the shelter to see what other little waif we could find, and we met BooBear. Unsettled from a chaotic puppyhood, he had no sense of security, no idea what it was like to belong or be loved. We're such suckers for the ones no one else wants—above our door should hang a sign beginning: "Give us your tired, your poor... your wretched refuse...." They're so happy when they finally have a place to call their own, and as soon as we met BooBear, we agreed to adopt him.

A true rag-bag pup, Boo's appearance inspired me to write this story about how he came to be:

As the long day in the workshop drew to a close, God sat back with a weary but satisfied smile. Hundreds had been assembled—a good day's work. But a survey of the leftover pieces, scattered around the work table and floor, revealed enough for one more.

The leftover creations were always the best ones; not the prettiest or the most noble-looking, but somehow just special.

Collecting the legs and body, God wondered if waiting until tomorrow would be better, to see what other parts might be available. This body—too long and too deep in the chest, and broad across the shoulders—would be hard for the slender legs to support. The legs were long enough, but fine-boned, with thin toes and nails.

"Well, he'll be able to cover some ground, anyway," God chuckled, sticking the pieces together.

With a wry smile, God gently picked up the head: "Not the prettiest face I've ever done." The forehead was too broad, the eyes wide-set above a longish, narrow nose. Floppy, soft ears hung heart-shaped on each side. The head was really a bit small for the body but big enough that it made the legs look even more outbalanced, as if the whole package would tip over without hesitation. Oh, well. On it went.

"I know I saw it somewhere," God mumbled, rummaging around among the workbench tools, searching for the tail. It was a sorry-looking one. "I must have been really tired when I made this. Or maybe I took the tip and used it somewhere else. But it'll have to do."

Nearly all of them were pointed, some long, some short, fat or skinny, but pointed at the end. Not this tail. It was short and fat like a sausage, with no taper at all, as thick at the end as it was at the base. God stuck it on, then stood back to observe the result. Somehow, the stocky tail balanced the body. But the whole thing was still a motley mix.

"Nope, he'll never win any beauty contests, that's for sure." This one would need a very special soul.

With gentle hands God drew the little face close, looked deep into the dark eyes, and puffed life into the creation. Soul light came shining up; the stumpy tail gave a tentative wag. God smiled.

"There you are, my little man, one of my finest ever. Go now and bring joy. Always be happy."

God opened the door, releasing another one into the world.

Arriving at yet another new home, BooBear was bewildered at first by all the MüFarm activity, and overwhelmed by his brothers. The uncertainty showed in his eyes, so we gave him time and space to find himself, letting him ease into the pack. Having never received much love or attention, he was hesitant when we gave him cuddles, which was hard for us—a pup who didn't know how to respond to affection broke our hearts. It would take time, but he'd come around.

Breed-wise, he was a guessing game. There was a lot of hound, probably some Beagle, and, since he was solid black from quirky head to stumpy tail, we suspected some Lab, too. The hound showed clearly in his love of hunting; he'd put his nose to the ground, pick up a scent, and run, oblivious to roadways, property boundaries, and the "come" command.

Even after several weeks, he still didn't grasp the concept of staying with us so we kept him on a tie-out line when outside (since fencing was unaffordable), and hiked with him on a long leash. Boo's young-pup energy wanted to join in the pack play and zoomies, but off-line time lasted only until he picked up a scent, and then off he went—so it was back to the tie-out. It was a difficult balance: we needed to keep him safe, but what kind of life would he have without freedom?

Knowing his shuttled-around past, it hurt to think of finding him yet another home. Plus, we were lifers—when we committed to a dog, it was forever. But were we the right home for Boo? I talked to Sarina about the possibility of us fostering him to see if she could find a home where he'd safely have some running room. She was disappointed (we were, too); he was starting to come out of his shell and uprooting him again would not be good.

Several days later, I was taking a break from chores when Boo came and stood in front of me, holding my gaze: *Please, don't send me away again.* Somehow, he'd sensed what we were thinking. My heart made the decision.

"MüFarm is your home now," I promised him, and he allowed a gentle hug. We told Sarina we'd give BooBear the best life we could, forever.

Although finally adopted, he didn't really feel like part of the pack for a good six months; none of our other adoptees had taken nearly so long to settle in. For human children, the sense of home and family security shapes them for life; Boo taught us how important it is for dogs, too. And he turned out to be such a character! Food was his driving force and he was always on the lookout for treats or stray crumbs. Second only to food was sleep. Boo loved a good nap, snuggling himself into one of several round, fleece-covered beds. Each morning, instead of getting up and stretching like his brothers, he'd roll on his back, twisting side to side with soft play-growls of pleasure.

"Wiggly worm, wiggly worm, BooBoo doin' wiggly worm!" I'd laugh, which made him roll around even more.

Mornings on MüFarm were always raucous. In addition to the smoothie-fruit madness, for some reason Shaman had turned howling into a daily routine, and Boo would join in with his unique howl-bark combination. The nose-to-the-sky concept was beyond him and even watching his brothers didn't help. It was just Boo's way, quirky and cute.

Then the rowdiness would begin, and when inside, they'd usually play wherever we were, crashing into our feet and legs. About half the weight of his brothers, Boo was more nimble and would flop over, belly-up and feet flailing, before jumping up, spinning around, and barking wildly. Learning how to play didn't take him long. At the dog park Boo was in heaven, running and playing, chasing and tumbling, his howl-bark distinct amid the chaos. Then he'd break away on his own, rambling the fence line, sniffing and marking, enjoying the freedom to do as he pleased.

But Boo's favorite activity by far was hiking. It didn't matter where. On his long leash-line, he'd wind his way through field and woods, stopping every two or three feet to sniff, analyzing every smell. When on a scent, all else vanished from his world: he wouldn't hear us call him, and he'd ignore his brothers unless they got too close to whatever he was hunting. Neither Rosko nor Shaman were serious hunters and after Red died our groundhog population returned. Boo went nuts! When he spotted one I'd let him loose, knowing he wouldn't go anywhere, and he'd sit, intently watching the hole, waiting for the critter to appear. But unlike Sammi and Red, BooBear had no patience. Rustling in the hole set him off, barking and frantically digging at the entrance, flinging dirt everywhere and scaring the critter deep into the burrow. It was a futile effort but kept him busy—until one memorable day he actually caught one.

Boo's sun-drenched nap by the barn turned into a frenzy of barking—*I've spied a groundhog!*—and, unclipped, he headed straight for the edge of the field, cornering a young one next to the fire pit. Surprised, he wasn't sure what to do next, lunging toward it and jumping back when the critter bared its teeth. It turned into an hours-long project, and when the barking finally stopped, Boo was lying by the barn, guarding the dead critter, so proud of himself. While he loved the thrill of the chase, his strategy remained the same and he never became a very savvy hunter, always trying to bark them to death rather than attacking.

HOME AT LAST: 2010

Whatever Lab ancestry Boo carried, he certainly did *not* inherit the swimming/water-loving gene. He hated anything that made him wet—lakes, creeks, baths—and he'd hold it for hours rather than go outside in the rain. Winter cold wasn't high on his list, either, since his coat under-fluff wasn't very thick. Indoors, he wanted to be covered up when he slept, which I discovered when my little fuzzy bathroom rug went missing. It, and Boo, were on the futon in my sewing room. Kevin wasn't home, so evidently Boo had snitched the rug, jumped up on the futon, and covered himself up. If he wanted it that much he could have it! The rug was his favorite "blanket" until one day at the Goodwill store I bought a bright, lime-green, fleece throw, printed with big black spiders. He loved it. From then on, after Boo picked his spot for the evening, we'd bundle him in the spider blanket. Once covered, he wouldn't move all night.

He didn't carry the Lab fetch gene, either, ignoring toys, balls, and the games his brothers played. The plush animals only interested him if they had plastic eyes or noses, and he'd spend hours chewing them off, leaving the poor, mangled creature for me to stitch up. More than once, with bare feet, I stepped on a forgotten chunk of plastic.

CHAPTER 13
Home: 2010

poppa

From the moment I met him, his gaze followed me everywhere, showing a patient knowledge; maybe his old soul knew me before, in some other time and place, and he wanted to belong to me again. His eyes were clouded by cataracts but they still held a wise calmness and deep understanding, as if he'd seen it all before and worried about nothing.

Ignoring my #1 rule—that I should *not* volunteer at adoption events—in August 2010, I helped at the shelter and met one of the new arrivals. Sarina had picked him up as a stray and named him Poppa, guessing his age at 11 or 12. He was a sweet, friendly old guy, but no one adopted him, and as I left the event he whined and pulled at his leash, trying to follow me. Obviously, he had me pegged! Boo had only been with us a short time, but Kevin and I had the "room for one more" discussion, the pack gave Poppa their sniff of approval and we brought him home. But what came next was completely unexpected.

As Poppa stepped from the car it was immediately clear he knew exactly where he was, as if he'd lived on MüFarm before. In the yard, there was none of the "running around sniffing everything" sense of disorientation and excitement, and inside he walked through each room slowly: *Ah, yes, it's just as I remember it.* Everything was familiar to him. We'd never seen anything like it.

Poppa must have been someone's pet; he was housebroken and even at his advanced age, he could hold it all day while we were at work. His initial vet visit showed no heart or intestinal worms, and his weight was ideal. Someone had taken good care of him. A 65-pound muttly mix of who-knew-what, he was square and solid with a broad head, Lab ears, and a big, shiny black nose. His short, luxurious coat was a rusty red, each hair dipped in black, and his heavy tail was dotted with a tiny black tip.

In addition to cataracts, Poppa had some gray on his muzzle and front paws, a spry energy that wore out quickly, and a little stiffness in his gait. His age and infirmities meant he was no threat to the pecking order so Rosko, Shaman, and Boo accepted him easily.

From the beginning, there was no need to keep him on a tie-out line or leash. He never left the yard and his eyes followed us closely. On hikes he tagged along behind the pack, moving at his own slow pace. Like Müddha, Poppa was a loner, a background pup who slipped quietly into our lives and activities, so undemanding he was barely there and whether indoors or out, he stayed to himself. The only time he joined the pack was during the daily howl, chiming in with a deep-from-the-belly sound, his special contribution to all the noise.

Neither toys nor rowdy pack play interested Poppa and he was content to doze in the warm sun or the shade of the lollipop tree, gazing out across the field, watching nothing in particular. He'd earned the right to do as he pleased and pass his retirement years peacefully.

One activity he *loved* was swimming. Avoiding the other dogs at the Alum Creek dog beach, Poppa spent most of his time in the lake, easing his hip arthritis and cooling off. He normally stayed where he could touch the bottom; when he did venture into deep water he was a strong swimmer, keeping up easily with Shaman and Rosko. But he was not a fetcher, and was happy to cruise quietly through the water.

Through 2011, as Poppa aged and his eyesight deteriorated we watched him carefully, especially at the dog park. By late August, we'd started him on pain medication for his arthritis, but he was getting grumpy and intolerant of the other dogs, so it was safer to keep him separated. All the activity overwhelmed him but he still wanted to swim and his legs needed the exercise. One day, with Kevin in charge of the other three, Poppa and I explored outside the dog park and discovered a tiny strip of beach, sloping gently down to the water.

On his own, away from the chaos, Poppa would swim back and forth or stand in the cool, chest-deep water, enjoying his private little spot. Watching him, I'd wonder about his past—like Lapsi, he'd appeared from nowhere, finding his way to MüFarm and attaching himself to us, happily following along wherever we went. A gentle behind-the-ear scratch, a full tummy, and a soft place to sleep were all he wanted.

By late summer 2012, the economy had stabilized and I took a position back in the corporate world, organizing a digital library at a Fortune 500 company in the banking industry. The office was in Columbus so I was back to making the long trek each day, but I didn't mind; I liked the job and the work was challenging, utilizing all my skills and demanding new ones. Plus, most of my new colleagues were dog lovers and among my team, scattered remotely around the world, were many other animal people. Team calls always started with shared stories and pictures of our pets. With my research skills, I became the go-to person for information on different pet conditions and symptoms, providing my team with online resources and research reports; it was the least I could do in memory of Red.

CHAPTER 14
A Little Secret: 2012

spanky

His eyes were bright, with a patience and trust rare in an abandoned dog, and a resolute but wary hopefulness: *Do you want me?*

A note to the one who left him:
In case you were wondering, here's what happened to the little dog you abandoned in Columbus back in the fall of 2012.

Before hitting the road home from work, Kevin made a quick restroom stop at a local park—but what karma drew him there, on that day, at that time? When he drove in, the park was empty and the little dog was right where you'd left him, tied to the signpost with his tennis ball at his side. Kevin watched for a long time, waiting to see if someone would come back, but it was moving toward evening and there was no way he'd drive off and leave the dog alone.

I've worked with animal rescues before so I'm unforgiving of people who dump animals when they no longer want them. There's not much excuse for it when there are abundant shelters, rescue groups, and humane organizations. It's pretty cold-hearted to tie a dog, walk away, and leave it to chance. I don't know how you could do it. But Kevin tends to be more tolerant; he thinks you really wanted to keep him but for some reason you couldn't. Did you know he was sick? Could you not afford to care for him? Maybe you gave up trying to housebreak him. Maybe it broke your heart to leave him there. But maybe not.

Were you watching from somewhere close by, hidden behind a tree? Did you care enough to at least make sure he wasn't left all alone in the dark? We'll never know, but will always wonder. Into the car he went, whisked off to a new life.

October 3, 2012: Kevin arrived home. "Wait until you see what's in the car," he called out. A familiar strategy—I've used it myself.

A LITTLE SECRET: 2012

"He's so little!" I said, as my heart melted.

To us, any pup under 30 pounds is small. Then I noticed his eyes, filled with pure love and innocence. But I could see something else there, too. Something I couldn't put my finger on. It was as if he held a little secret.

Grumpy Poppa was in the house, but Shaman, Rosko and Boo surrounded the car, curious about the newcomer, and much wagging, sniffing, and barking ensued. The little one returned the greeting, showing no fear—his confidence was unusual for a stray—and once the ruckus was over, we walked him around the yard. He was a friendly little guy and unbearably adorable, a blend of Pomeranian and Corgi from head to tail. Long, fluffy, blond fur covered his short legs and long body, draping from his tummy, tail, and hind legs. As he trotted along the hair swung from side to side—I called it his Happy Pants. A thick mane ringed his neck and his long tail curved up, halfway between a tight Pom curl and a natural Corgi tail; from the very first day, we dubbed him a PomaCorgian.

Our pack had already eaten, so I took him inside for dinner, then walked him through the house. He wasn't housetrained and was intact—a double whammy—so he wanted to mark everything. Maybe that's why he'd been abandoned. Back outside we let him wander and follow along with the pack, exploring the gardens and barn. For a city dog, the rural scents must have been extra exciting. His day had started out with familiar smells, people, and voices but now he was in a completely different world—everything was new.

Change is exhausting, so we brought the old-faithful airline crate up from the basement and got him settled down for the night. As I fell asleep, I wondered if his former family was thinking of him. Was there a child somewhere, wondering what had happened to his friend? Did they pick up the lonely food bowl, hang the leash out of sight, and put the little bed away? Did anyone think of him at all? I was angry, and sad. What possessed them to leave a dog alone in the world where anything terrible could have happened to him? It makes no sense, but it happens all the time. I was so glad his path crossed ours. My last thought of the day: he was lucky.

After breakfast we introduced him to Poppa, who was not at all amused and took an immediate dislike to the intruder. (In his decline, Poppa didn't have much tolerance for anything and was even grumpy toward the established pack.) Poppa didn't move very fast anymore, but he surprised us by growling and charging at the new boy; Kevin scooped him up out of harm's way, and from then on we kept them separated.

The Maple Run clinic scanned the little guy but he wasn't chipped, so I spent the rest of the morning calling shelters and posting "found dog" information on several websites, with no luck. During an afternoon walk around the yard, he had terrible diarrhea and the vet suspected parvovirus, so we went back to the clinic to find out for sure. Parvovirus is very contagious (our pupz had been vaccinated against it long ago), so the vet techs came out to the car to swab him—he tested positive. This was serious.

Dr. Mooney outlined our three choices: $350 would treat him in the clinic, requiring total isolation and intensive care for a week; for $80, we could treat him at home with subcutaneous IV fluids four times a day and oral antibiotics for secondary infection; or we could euthanize him, which was not a legitimate option—he deserved a fighting chance. The $350 was out of reach, so right there in the back of the car in the parking lot, they showed me how to do the IV and told me what to expect, including the strong possibility he might not survive. Home we went with a box of IV needles, plastic tubing, saline bags, and lots of determination that he'd be fine. We'd detected the virus very early, improving his chances.

It was a crazy week. Rosko and Boo took the upheaval in stride, while Shaman worried over Poppa and supervised the parvo treatment. Between Poppa's failing health and the little one's needs, we were all busy. The new boy was starting to feel the effects of the virus—high temperature, no appetite, no water consumption—and he looked pathetic. The IV-drip schedule defined the days and he'd lie quietly in Kevin's lap on the kitchen floor while I held the needle in place. The fluids were barely maintaining him but he was a little fighter, clamping his mouth shut and refusing most of the antibiotics. It was frustrating but made us all the more certain he'd pull through. After each IV treatment I'd sit on the couch holding him to my chest, gently petting and talking to him; he was so lethargic and sick. If I wasn't holding him Kevin was, and as the days went by we watched and waited for signs of improvement. We began calling him Little Buddy.

Toward the end of the week, in one large, vile-smelling explosion, he shed the virus and all that remained in his system. As awful as it was, he'd turned the corner—but until he began eating and drinking on his own, the IV treatments continued. He was very weak and had lost several pounds (a sizable amount on his little frame), but at last, he took a few shaky steps to the water bowl. Even though he didn't actually drink, we were ecstatic; simply showing interest was a big deal.

But as Little Buddy improved, Poppa fell apart. During most of the parvo treatment I'd worked from home, but returned from Columbus on Friday to find the living room a total disaster. Poppa had lost control of his bowels and walked right through the mess, tracking it all over the floor before collapsing in it. I helped him outside, got the other pupz taken care of, then donned rubber gloves and tackled the floor. Kevin arrived home and we carefully cleaned poor Poppa, but he was in pain, growling and snapping as we tried to help him; his message was clear and I called the vet to come the next morning. After making Poppa comfortable and administering Little Buddy's IV, we fed everyone, set our exhaustion aside, and tried to give Rosko, Shaman, and Boo some decent exercise.

Since the shelter staff was like family, we always let them know when one of their adoptees was at the end, and Crystal came to say goodbye to Poppa. He was so out of sorts she could only sit next to him on the porch, talking to him softly through loving tears.

"It's hard," she said. "I want to hug and cuddle him, but I have to respect his space and how he feels." I understood—I could still touch him, but cuddles were out of the question.

As they had for Sammi, Eric and Becky made the drive from Oberlin that evening. Eric shared a special bond with Poppa, but even though Poppa was mellow from pain medication, he still wouldn't allow Eric to pet him. In the slanted sunlight, they sat together on the grass, with Eric as close as Poppa would allow; he was already separating himself, beginning his journey.

In the morning, on a soft bed in the three-season room, we gave him the sedative, comforting him as the pain faded and his head came to rest on his paws for the final sleep. The vet arrived and Poppa left our lives.

Wherever he'd come from and whatever he'd endured, he passed over at home, surrounded by love. Poppa rests for all time where he knew he belonged, on MüFarm next to those gone before. His lantern candle burned a long time, until the wax melted away and there was nothing left. Sail along, old soul. Thank you for coming into our lives, for teaching us to be content with the small things, and reminding us to simply relax sometimes and watch the world go by.

Eating and drinking on his own now, our Little Buddy was well on his way to a complete recovery. His appetite returned, he gained back the lost pounds, and his personality quickly emerged. From his Corgi genes it was *very* apparent he'd inherited the intelligence, as well as the stubborn independence; he was quite the little rascal, so we named him Spanky.

With his health issues and neuter surgery behind him, we started Spanky's training, helped along by the behavior of the other three. He followed their lead, doing as the big boys did, which worked out well, most of the time. BooBear wasn't much into doing tricks, but he loved treats and taught Spanky the fine art of begging. From Rosko and Shaman, he picked up "sit," "shake," and even "roll over," twisting his long body and short legs to flip himself.

Spanky's Pomeranian curiosity and feistiness perfectly matched Rosko's bold orneriness, and they became a real pair, playing with the same level of intensity Rosko had enjoyed with Shadow. Curious about everything, they followed each other around, always looking for—and finding—something to get into. Even on dry days they managed to get dirty, digging up mole holes and rolling around out in the pasture. On hot days they were constantly in the pup pool, dirty, wet, and happy.

But while Spanky learned good behavior from Rosko, he also picked up some of his monkeyshines—they hung together like two bad boys at the back of the classroom. Loitering in the yard when they were supposed to come in was a favorite, pretending not to hear us calling, glancing our way as they sniffed and sauntered toward the house.

"Bye, Mom's going in!" I'd yell, closing the door behind me.

That always brought them running, especially Spanky. When I opened the door he'd be plastered up against it, as if he'd been abandoned once again; he was becoming a Mom's boy, always at my feet or wanting to be on my lap.

Like Sammi, Spanky brought his own twist to all the old-standard games. Way at the bottom of the toy bucket he discovered a long-forgotten small rubber ball, but traditional fetch was no fun—he required me to bounce it against the floor so he could jump up and catch it. One day I tossed it into the upper hallway, thinking he'd run up and bring it back down. Instead, he ran up, tossed it from the top step, and watched while it bounced down to me for another throw. Sometimes, he'd put it down by his feet then sit next to it, waiting.

"Make it come down," I prompted. To my surprise, he pushed it with his nose until it rolled off the edge and down the steps. This became his favorite game.

Spanky also got a kick out of Mouse, and the two of them would roll his ball around, batting it back and forth until Spanky's high-pitched, frustrated bark demanded I retrieve it from under the furniture. Always enthralled by the pupz' tails, Mouse found Spanky's Happy Pants irresistible and she'd pull and jump on the hair, which earned her Spanky's *OK, that's enough,* snarl-growl. But in spite of their spits and spats, when playtime was over they'd curl up on the couch, Mouse's head on Spanky's soft, furry tummy.

Except for his physical size, everything about Spanky was big: his bark, his attitude, and his energy. At the dog park he played mostly with the big dogs—Millie, a Great Dane, was his favorite pal—and he looked at those his own size as if they were aliens. Even with his short legs, he was extremely fast and when the chase was on, he outran nearly every other dog, big or small.

To channel his high energy, I enrolled him in a local agility club; the mental focus kept him sharp, and the running helped tire him out. He loved it so much I set up a small practice course in the backyard with PVC-pipe jumps, an old fabric play tunnel, and a set of weave poles. It was such fun, Rosko got in on it, too. Of course, he had his own ideas about how it should be done, crashing his bufflehead and body right through the jumps instead of going over, then rolling on the ground to show how extremely cute he was. Too big for the tunnel, he tried anyway, getting stuck and dragging it around—Rosko never took anything seriously! Any real Spanky training was done with Rosko in the house.

At agility trials, Spanky could hardly wait until it was his turn, and he was so fast I could barely keep up with him as we ran the course. But after several months, his Corgi stubborn-streak kicked in and he started to run only when he wanted to. Even the high-value treat rewards didn't help. The jumps, tunnel, and elevated dog-walk were his favorite obstacles—he liked the high vantage point of the dog-walk so much that he'd stop at the top and refuse to budge. He didn't care for the weave poles and would sit down rather than run through them, which was very cute but disqualified him from any competition. Eventually, he lost interest in it completely, so I stashed the training equipment in the shed. It was fun while it lasted.

Spanky played with anyone and everyone, but if he was tired or frightened and needed comfort, he turned to Shaman. Spanky's boldness had its limits and loud sounds, like hunters' gunfire or thunder, turned him into a trembling little mess. Shaman the Protector would gladly step in. And, after a long day of play activities, they became cuddle buddies, spending many winter evenings curled up on the big bed in front of the fire, their blond coats blending together.

But Spanky's favorite spot was on the couch with Mom, his little body warm up against me as I read or watched TV, and the bond that had formed between us during his parvo recovery grew stronger. As the months passed, I saw in his personality the best traits of all our previous pupz, embodied somehow within his small being: he was determined, curious, creative, bold yet cautious, independent yet fiercely loyal, and extremely smart. But above all, a deep understanding lived in his eyes and frequently he'd sit gazing at me intently. There was something he was trying to tell me. Then one day, he did.

With a fire going one cold winter afternoon, I rested on the couch under a fleece blanket with Spanky nestled in the crook of my body. We dozed, then slept. Suddenly, I awoke with a start to find Spanky sitting up in front of me, staring into my eyes.

"Oh my God, it's Red in there!" Like a flash of truth and with a surety in my soul, I saw Red staring back at me through Spanky's eyes. I suddenly understood what I'd felt the first time I saw Spanky, the secret he held for me. I had asked Red to come back, and there he was, returned across the beyond. The closed place in my heart reopened and Spanky stepped in. Staring back into his eyes, I nodded, and the understanding passed between us. My soul pup was with me again.

While hunting and killing were not activities we encouraged, ever since Sammi we'd accepted that for some dogs, it's part of their nature. As it had with Sammi, fast movement set Spanky off and his Corgi DNA kept him busy during the winter, digging with Rosko for mice hiding under the snow. But while Rosko enjoyed just finding the nests, Spanky decimated them.

Tenacious and oh-so-quick, once on a scent Spanky never gave up, running down and outmaneuvering whatever he was after. Calling or yelling at him to stop was a waste of effort; his focus was completely on the prey. By summer 2013, we'd switched our farm-field acreage from corn and soybeans to hay, and on one mid-summer hike, Spanky spotted a squirrel in the freshly mowed field, out in the open, far from any trees. The chase was on. His herding instinct kicked in and as the squirrel zig-zagged, frantic to find something to climb, Spanky anticipated the pattern and cut it off. When it ran straight for the tree line, it was game over, and Spanky trotted proudly back to me, carrying the dead squirrel.

Various small critters found their way into the house now and then; no squirrels, but the occasional frog, toad, or skink, and many mice. Traps, and the cats, kept the mouse population semi-contained, but in an old house there was no way to keep them out, and every so often one found its way to the main floor. What is it about a half-ounce of brown fur that makes pupz go so crazy?! One afternoon I investigated a ruckus in the dining room and found them all in a frenzied blur, chasing a little field mouse around the baseboard, climbing over one another and knocking the chairs askew. When the mouse tried to jump up the wall, Spanky was on it immediately, walking away from the fray with its tail hanging between his clenched jaws: *I got him, Mom, you're safe now!*

"OK, outcha go!" Banished to the yard in case the mouse was crafty enough to escape, I put the dining room back in order. Forever after, if Spanky even *thought* he heard a mouse inside, he'd run around in hunt mode until he caught it or it managed to get away.

The three-season room was upended next. At first I couldn't spot what Spanky was after, but he was scrabbling around, barking wildly, and crawling under the furniture, so obviously some evil monster was on the loose. Then, a flash of tiny, blue-tailed skink darted from beneath the glider. Spanky snapped, catching the lizard by the tail, which it promptly shed, then the lucky critter skittered out under the door. The tail writhed for a minute before Spanky lost interest, but he was busy for the next few hours, sure the skink was still around somewhere. Between the four pupz, there was never a dull moment.

After Gunner died, MüFarm didn't see another horse until fall 2014, when I bought Ramsey, a big, sturdy, Tennessee Walker trail horse, dark bay—almost black—with a big white star. Boo, Shaman, and Rosko were used to horses, but Spanky was intimidated and wary at first, worrying over Mom up in the saddle. And when Ramsey was in the pasture, we watched Spanky carefully. His herding instinct brought him too close to Ramsey's feet at times, but he was smart and quick enough to get out of the way and soon learned to respect Ramsey's space.

Spanky took over Red and Müddha's barn duties, supervising the stall cleaning, and hunting mice under the hay. Ramsey round-up time was Spanky's favorite chore and as dusk moved in we'd head for the pasture. A clang of the lead-line clasp against the metal gate brought Ramsey's head up, and as he started toward me, Spanky would take off to meet him. Across the pasture they'd come, 1,200-pound Ramsey respectfully allowing 25-pound Spanky to herd him in.

Ramsey loved the pupz so we began our rides together, first going around the hay field and then venturing down the road and into Penlan Park. On his line, Boo hiked along with Kevin, and while Rosko and Spanky raced ahead, we paced ourselves for Shaman. He was 10 now and on medication for an enlarged heart and hip arthritis, so he moved more slowly, joining Boo on his wanderings.

Shaman's morning howl-fest was now punctuated with coughing as the stress on his ailing heart took its toll, and his eyes said he knew his body was failing. In a late October picture, he lies in a pile of brown, crunchy leaves, his worried, all-knowing eyes staring into the camera. His brow is wrinkled and his graying muzzle frames a little frown: *Mom, who will watch over everything when I'm gone?* Even years later, the picture still breaks my heart.

Neema — November 2014

Little Neema was the worst neglect case we'd ever seen. We were returning from a cold November morning walk when my cell phone rang—it was the dog warden. A kind man had brought a little stray into Dr. Mooney's practice that morning, and her office had called the shelter. The dog needed intense, hands-on care and Sarina asked if we could foster. Out came the old dog crate once again, and Shaman perked up at the prospect of a new patient to look after.

Neema arrived wrapped in a warm blanket and the white, furry face peeking out was Pomeranian with big eyes; small, pointed ears; and a dark red nose. Then Sarina put her on the floor and removed the blanket. We were horrified! There was nothing to her. She was literally skin and bones and weighed only seven pounds. Her coat was mostly clipped away, showing bare patches of red, irritated skin where mats had been, and her joints revealed pressure sores. Each rib was clearly visible and her spine and hip bones nearly poked through her skin. With her tail tucked between her legs, she stood unsteadily on her little feet, hunched up and trembling.

Over the next few days we kept her warm, eased her tummy back into regular meals, and made sure she got a little exercise, tottering around the house and yard wearing a toasty pink sweater. But she spent most of her time in the crate, sleeping in the fleece; she was on the edge of life but still had the will to try.

Shaman was smitten with her and would lie next to the crate, supervise her feeding, and walk along when she went outside. As she gained weight and strength he guarded her, keeping the others out of her way while she explored the house. It gave him new purpose and diverted us all from his health worries. Rosko was curious, but Neema couldn't play yet so he lost interest. BooBear ignored her, and while Spanky was jealous of the attention she was getting, he was also gentle, perhaps remembering he once needed help, too.

Neema was old, her teeth were very bad, and we suspected she was mostly or completely deaf. Placing a special-needs senior would be a challenge—she would only go to someone Sarina and I trusted—but I started putting feelers out, emailing her picture and story to my dog-loving friends.

Jean responded right away. She was part of my original group of dog-rescuing co-workers and, like me, she had a huge soft spot for the old ones. Once Neema was strong enough, Jean would adopt her.

Neema was a feisty old lady. With regular food and exercise she continued to improve, her skin began to heal, and the angry red patches faded to a healthy pink, sprouting little stubbles of hair. After a few weeks with us, she was out of danger, her adoption was finalized, and Jean picked her up.

Most of Neema's teeth had to be extracted so she was put on a mashed diet; she eventually reached her ideal weight and her coat grew in completely. Jean renamed her Sophie and sent regular progress reports as she returned to health—my favorite picture shows a happy Sophie with bright eyes and a thick, beautiful white coat. Side-by-side with her "before" picture, it's nearly impossible to believe she's the same dog.

Sophie was definitely a Pomeranian, a little princess who loved being the center of attention, and Jean completely spoiled her. Sophie wasn't much for toys, but she had a better wardrobe than some children, several soft beds, regular vet care, and plenty of food. But even the best care and all Jean's love couldn't wipe away the neglect Sophie's little body had suffered; over her last year, she became incontinent and struggled to get around. In early June 2017, she passed away in Jean's loving arms.

The 2014 holidays were as happy as we could make them. Shaman's declining health kept us home so I went overboard at the Goodwill store, buying three toys for each pup, and the sounds of barking, ripping paper, and new squeaky toys filled the house. Once the packages were open, they all swapped toys until each found their favorites. BooBear homed in on the chew bones, while Spanky made off with several toys, building up a little hoard behind the chair. Rosko ignored the toys and rolled around on the huge pile of shredded paper. Shaman still loved his Green Fish the best, and several years before I'd bought him a second one. Every Christmas I'd wrap one of them up so he could rediscover his little buddy. Once he found it, he was content.

Kept out of reach among the chaos were gifts for the cats, and Mouse watched from the safety of the couch; she'd enjoy her treats and catnip mice later. Inside the back porch was a warm box for the barn cats, Laverne and Shirley, and on a whim I'd bought them a large, white, stuffed cat to snuggle, setting it on the shelf next to their bed.

Who knows what gets into a pup's head, why they do certain things and where funny little behaviors come from? After our Christmas-morning walk, as we came in through the back porch, Spanky spied the stuffed cat up on the shelf and stared at it intently, wagging wildly.

"No, silly boy, that's not a real kitty," I said, opening the back door.

Spanky looked at me, looked back at the cat, then he stood up on his hind legs, grabbed it by the tail, and pulled it down. He was so excited, rolling on it before carrying it into the house: *It's mine now!* And so KatKat became Spanky's absolute favorite toy—*no one* else was allowed to play with it. KatKat was half the size of Spanky himself and he carried it everywhere, holding his head high to avoid tripping on the tail. The toy became part of the greeting committee after work, and if a neighbor stopped by, Spanky ran to find it. When we went outside, KatKat came, too, and was sometimes left in the yard.

"Go find your KatKat." Unlike Bear, Spanky always remembered where he left it.

KatKat also became his security blanket—when Spanky was nervous or frightened, he'd lie next to Shaman, holding the toy in his mouth. In time, KatKat's white, plush fur slowly turned permanently brown where Spanky's mouth grabbed and held it. The plastic eyes both disappeared (thanks to Boo), and the nylon filament-line whiskers became bent and twisted from repeated trips through the washer and dryer. I've stitched up holes in the seams and reattached the tail once or twice. It's his forever-favorite toy.

After the holidays, Shaman deteriorated. Arthritis made it hard for him to get around and he was losing muscle tone in his back legs, becoming wobbly as he walked. Along with the stress on his heart, his liver numbers rose, his appetite fell, and although he didn't give up, he didn't show the fight and determination that Sammi had at the end. Using the Sammi strategy, we tempted Shaman with ground chicken and it worked for a while, but he ate slowly and, as we had with Bear, we sometimes picked the bowl up to save for later. Familiar with the stages by now, we'd learned the simple acceptance of each day. We understood the trust they put in us and our responsibility—to read their eyes and then be brave enough to do what they asked.

The Shammi Sunday dog-park schedule continued as long as Shaman was willing. He was a favorite at the park and everyone loved seeing him, following along with his ups and downs, offering condolences and advice. But our options were running out. Wearing Poppa's warm, fleece-lined jacket, Shaman made his last dog-park trip on January 25, 2015. On a bench in the bright winter sun he laid by my feet as I sat, just enjoying being with him. Gazing out across the snowy park, I pictured him running and playing, and in his eyes I saw the same far-away remembering. Pulling my glove off, I stroked his head. At my touch he looked up.

"Yes, buddy, I know. It was the best of times." His tail thumped the snow.

Overnight into January 27th was a hard time for all on MüFarm. Shaman's system gave him trouble and we were up and down with him throughout the night. He looked away in shame as I cleaned the floor then gently washed him off.

"Don't worry, sweet boy, Mom will fix it." I held his face between my hands and our eyes met as I tried to reassure him.

In the morning he rallied, and although he didn't eat, he still orchestrated the daily howl and took a slow walk around the yard. But he was turning inward. *It's time for me to go.*

The neighbors came to say goodbye and by early afternoon, exhausted from stress and broken sleep the night before, we built a fire and napped in the living room. With the pupz gathered around, Kevin sat with us as I laid next to Shaman on the big pup bed in front of the hearth, cradling him against me, and tucking Green Fish between his front paws. Spanky brought KatKat and curled against Shaman's tummy, very aware his brother and protector was beginning his journey.

Later, on his bed in front of the fire, Shaman left this life. Boo and Rosko laid close by, comforting our tears, but Spanky, so aware of the loss, stood and gently pawed Shaman's face, a soft whine crying in his chest. As the fire burned down, Kevin fed everyone and took them outside while I sat by our boy a little longer, remembering his first anxious weeks with us as he got to know his new home and family. He was young and strong then, searching for who he would become and where he belonged. He'd found it all on MüFarm, his special, happy place, his world to guard and protect. Our Guardian in Chief was gone—what an honor to have known him.

Aside from Lapsi, we'd buried our other pupz, returning their empty bodies to the soil of MüFarm while their souls journeyed onward. Even Lapsi was anchored on MüFarm, the dogwood tree guarding her ashes in the Memory Garden. But with Shaman's passing we began a new tradition, escorting his body for cremation, then lighting his lantern candle in the frosty evening. Frozen ground, and our aging backs, meant he'd stay with us, and when his ashes came back we placed the box, and Green Fish, on the dining room sideboard, touching them with love each time we passed. The strength of his spirit is forever on watch.

When Müsta passed away so many years before, we began a custom of keeping the last collar from each pup and hanging them all together on a hook in the coat closet. When the door opened, the tags jingled, and there they all were again: Müsta's dignified black band, Müddha's colorful nylon with red-hot chili peppers embroidered all around, the brown rolled-leather ones left by Sammi and Red. As we added new ones, the hook filled up until the collars dropped to the floor when the door opened. We added a third hook for Shaman's collar.

After a loss, the firsts of everything are incredibly hard. The first walk, first day, first week—the tears flow so easily. At feeding time, Shaman's empty bowl was huge but impossible to put away for a while. We listened for his paws on the hardwood floor, the sound of his bark mixed in with the pack, and, of course, the morning howl. The first morning, I was making the breakfast smoothies when Spanky began the soft woofs that had always followed Shaman's lead. The woofs became louder then he began the howl, Rosko and Boo joined in, and the joyous, mournful sound filled the house. Through tears, Kevin and I watched them carry on Shaman's tradition. Spanky was the new leader of the howls, taking over from his favorite brother.

The first Sunday, Spanky made sure we remembered, running to find KatKat and getting us moving: *Dad, Mom, it's Shammi Sunday!* All our dog-park friends supported us and it was good to be with those who understood the burden of the loss. As the pack zoomed around, we watched for Shaman, sure he was there somewhere, his young, playful self, joining in. Perhaps he was.

The pack felt Shaman's loss acutely. Maybe they missed being looked after, missed his constant presence, gone so suddenly. There was no discernable pack shift, no jockeying for dominance as with past losses, and even Rosko, the boldest and most independent of the three, was at loose ends. In the evenings, Spanky and KatKat laid on the bed near the fireplace where they'd shared many cozy nights with Shaman—they looked so lonely. The absence was heavy on us all, but each loss confirmed our belief in honoring them by saving another and, even so soon, we began thinking about an addition.

CHAPTER 15
Back to a Four-Pack: 2015

archie

His eyes were bright, mischievous, and full of questions: *You look like fun, who are you? Am I not the cutest boy ever? Don't you want to take me home?* I did.

The shelter's "adoptable dogs" page was bookmarked on my laptop and I checked it often, always on the lookout for needy pupz to share among my friends. About three weeks after Shaman left us, a picture appeared of a young pup who reminded me of Sammi. When we adopt, we usually go for older ones since they're harder to place, but something about this guy grabbed me. At the shelter we met Archie.

"Watch out! He's an excited pee-er!" Sarina warned, and, proving her point, Archie promptly rolled belly-up and sent out a stream of urine, somehow missing us all.

Picked up as a stray from a busy two-lane highway outside of Mount Gilead, he had no microchip or collar, and the shelter had received no calls from anyone looking for him. Once his stray-hold was up, he met the pack and we brought him home.

Probably a Husky/Golden Retriever mix, he was about seven months old, and his feet said that once he grew into them he'd be a big boy, around 70-80 pounds. His coat was like Sammi's except very light, almost white, with the same thick Husky-ness, and a fluffy tail curling up and over his back, carried high like a flag. Beautiful, toasty ears matched a generous sprinkling of freckles covering his nose, giving him extra character.

Since he was so young, his place in the pack was rock bottom and the others accepted him easily, although Rosko and Spanky were jealous. Archie was our first puppy since Müsta and we'd forgotten how much energy they had and how much attention they demanded. In the house, he was a wild man right away and feeding time was crazy as he jumped up against the countertop, pushing the others out of the way. Obedience training would start with the basics.

That first night, after our evening field hike and play we were all tired, except for Archie. At bedtime, we coaxed him into the large kennel with treats, secured the gate, then fell into bed, waiting for the barking, howling protests to begin. Blessed quiet; he slept soundly through the night.

Day one with Archie—time for a serious plan! The crate was clean, so he could hold it, but the excited peeing required a belly band in the house. Research on the condition said we should keep him as calm as possible (easier said than done), not get him overly excited (yeah, right), and pretty much ignore him when he did go—making a fuss would only make it worse. We did our best, and it worked well in conjunction with his housebreaking training. Within a few weeks he was on the regular pack schedule.

Archie was a good boy and eager to please. Every minute became a teaching moment and he learned that treats were forthcoming when he did as we asked. But until he learned the rules we restrained him at feeding time. Our eternal remodeling had made its way to the dining room/kitchen entryway, where old paneling had been torn out in preparation for drywall. Anchoring a hefty screw eye into an exposed wood stud, we attached a short tie-line and clipped it to Archie's collar; it worked perfectly. Since he was the low man in the pack, his bowl went down last and he was *not* happy about it—self-control is a tough one, but eventually he learned to sit and wait his turn.

The training was a good brush-up for everyone. Archie was a fast learner, but when he did something wrong, the others stared at him, aghast. Without our Red/Shaman Rat-out Patrol, Spanky stepped in to spot errant behavior and Archie didn't get away with much. The hard one for him was the "come" command. Archie shared Sammi's independent streak and stubbornness, and he tried our patience at times. Our old trick of walking away didn't work. Linda had moved away but Kim from the dog shelter was also a trainer and she got us all started in the right direction. Following the lead of his brothers, Archie was soon charging back when we called.

But teaching him not to chase Ramsey was another problem altogether; Archie was clueless about horses. On Archie's third day with us, I'd walked him on a leash down Turner Trail and Ramsey came over to nose him through the fence. At first Archie was just curious, but then he lunged, frightening Ramsey who galloped off, sending Archie into a frenzy. It was not good. We could not have a dog who chased horses.

As the weeks went by, Archie gave no indication he would ever get used to Ramsey, even with firm training. In the end, it was either send Archie back to the shelter, sell my horse, or resort to an electronic collar. Neither Kevin nor I wanted to collar him but we were out of options, so we consulted a highly recommended trainer, bought the equipment, and began the sessions. The idea was to use it only until Archie understood that Ramsey was totally off limits, then we could put the collar away forever. He caught on right away, but I've always been sorry we did it—even years later, he still shakes his head at the "leave it" command, in anticipation of the mild shock.

During his first months, we decided we really liked the name Archie. "He acts more like a Jughead," Kevin observed, but Archie was a better fit and much more dignified.

From the beginning, Spanky was his special buddy. Maybe it was because Spanky missed Shaman so much, but maybe Spanky simply loved Archie. Though a mismatch in size, their young-pup energy levels were the same and their play was over the top. Spanky was so short and quick that he could duck underneath his new brother, and Archie would lose track of him until Spanky popped up, grabbed Archie by his scruff-neck fur, and held on. Archie would then grab Spanky's tail, and on it went. Each knew how far to take it and when to let go.

One thing I missed was my solo time with Spanky; Archie and Rosko were jealous and so any playtime had to include them all. Playing Spanky's make-it-come-down game on the stairs was an invitation for Archie to grab the ball and run away with it. During Tug o' War I needed a toy in each hand so Archie could be in on it, too, while Rosko and Boo rolled around underfoot. But it was fun to play with them all, watching the competition and camaraderie as the pack evolved.

Archie quickly learned that leaving MüFarm on his own was a huge no-no, but after the fall harvest, long walks together over the neighbors' empty fields became a regular treat. Forbidden-field walks were *very* exciting! Somehow, the smells were much more special and we let the pupz ramble and hunt as long as they wanted, stopping for a good roll now and then. The stiff, dry crop-stubble made a great back scratcher and if there was something stinky, all the better.

Spanky's coat picked up all manner of field shrapnel and they all came home dirty, but very happy.

Winter field hikes were real exercise as the snow blew unimpeded across the open fields and drifts piled up in the swales. With 200 acres of open field, Rosko and Archie ran flat-out, plowing through the drifts, tumbling and rolling, making snow angels in the bright winter sun. Spanky played the Arctic fox, diving in headfirst and digging madly after the mice, his long hair collecting round, clumpy "snow hooters" between his front legs and along his tummy. Never the trailblazer, Boo ambled along in our footsteps, bundled in his winter jacket, sniffing intently at the deer tracks crisscrossing the field, following his nose wherever it led. Endless days in pup paradise.

By spring 2015, I was officially an orphan. Mom passed on in late March, fading peacefully away as Beth and I held her hands. Spanky had continued to make frequent visits with me, cheering Mom and the other residents, but there came a day when I called Beth: "Something is different about Mom."

On my next trip, I left Spanky home and made what turned out to be my final visit, spending the next several days with Mom. Surrounded by her children, she stopped eating and turned inward, beginning her journey. It was an odd feeling, like becoming unmoored; my last safe harbor gone forever. Somehow, she'd guided her children through the turmoil of the '60s and '70s, a world so changed for her that at times

I'm sure she must have wondered what to do with us. But she gave us all such a firm foundation, teaching by example with her quiet patience and kindness, that even throughout my wandering 20s I managed to stay grounded.

Mom's innate understanding and love included all children, not just her own. After she couldn't drive anymore, our outings would take twice as long as they should have, since she oohed and aahed over every baby and child and engaged each parent with sincere interest. She saw the good in every person and the potential in every child, valuing each as an individual. I learned this lesson but added my own twist—I saw the good and potential in every animal. Neither Kevin nor I have ever passed by any critter looking hurt or lost. A turtle about to cross the road brings the car to a screeching halt, and an injured animal means a trip to the vet, sometimes setting off a scramble to find the nearest wildlife rehab center.

There are those who don't understand, those who get a kick out of the "roadkill recipes" and the crunch of tiny bones under their tires. For them, I feel pity; there's a beauty lost and a piece of the heart missing. I'm glad Kevin and I are on the other side, feeling the joy and the connection. I'm even glad we can feel the pain of an animal deceased, whether it's a wild thing on the road, a poor stray, or a beloved pet. I'm sure Mom never anticipated where her lesson would lead me.

Beth and I catch ourselves now and then, saying a Momism or doing something we know would have earned us the patented Mom Look of Disapproval. But overall, I believe mom's children made her happy and she passed away knowing she'd done a good job. I like to think I was a good daughter, that I didn't worry her too much and she was pleased with me in the end, but there are things I wish I would have said or done, things I realized too late. In my heart, I speak to her often and thank her for being such a great mom. I should have said it more often in life.

I wish she'd given me, early on, more of a sense of self, a belief I could be something. But I understand now that finding my own way was more meaningful, something I needed to do on my own. She probably knew that. Now, it was up to me to sink or swim, succeed or fail, with no one's expectations to live up to but my own—which was actually harder.

The summer 2015 project was remodeling the back of the house. We insulated the former back porch and finished it off into The Café—a sunny breakfast room with a pass-through to the kitchen. Then we extended the porch roof line and added a large mudroom, mostly to make taking care of the pupz easier. It included lots of cupboards and coat hooks, a big boot box, a utility sink for cleaning up after gardening, and, best of all, a floor-level mop-sink big enough to accommodate Rosko.

To test it out for size before construction was finished, I coaxed Rosko into the tub and asked him to sit. His drooping ears and wary, resigned eyes said, *Oh, this is not good!* Swimming and pool play were great fun but baths were definitely not a favorite!

BACK TO A FOUR-PACK: 2015

Kevin and I loved the mudroom for so many reasons and, aside from the washtub, the pupz loved it too, especially Rosko, who napped on the cool concrete floor in the warm weather. We called it the Rosko Room.

At summer's end, I became a full-time teleworker, happily saying goodbye to the Columbus commute and rush-hour grind. The pupz loved the change, too: *Oh, boy, Mom's home all the time now!* Lunchtime meant field walks, then they'd all pile into my office, serenading me with snores while in the living room below, our collection of antique mantel clocks bonged away the hours. When the chimes struck four, it was food time, but Spanky and Archie would begin stirring about 3:15, standing up against my chair and trying to con me.

"No, it's another 45 minutes. Too early for dinner." They'd lie back down, trying again at around 3:45, hoping persistence would pay off. It never did.

My former commute time became playtime and as the days shortened we took long evening walks while it was still light. Following the well-worn path through the hay field, the pupz meandered back and forth across the trail sniffing out nests buried near the ground. As the mice scattered, Spanky and Archie chased, and usually whatever they were after came out on the short end.

The hikes were Boo's happy time, the highlight of his days, and his stumpy tail never stopped wagging as we strolled through the field behind the others. Our pace was leisurely, following Boo's nose as he snuffled along, going into a digging, barking frenzy when he found a nest. After the hay was cut and baled, the remaining nests were easy targets. Sadly, the baling process also killed a few critters, caught in the tall grass before they could escape the blades, and the pupz joyously ground the stinky carcasses into their fur from head to tail. The Rosko Room wash-tub paid for itself the first year.

Our walks always ended in the orchard and the fallen apples kept Rosko, Spanky, and Archie busy while Boo supervised my evening barn chores. Rosko taught Archie to love apples, but we carefully picked up the brown ones before the yellow jackets moved in—we discovered the hard way that Archie was allergic to bee venom. One evening, I found a couple of nice apples. "Archie, want these?" I asked, as I bowled one across the yard.

Oh boy! A new game! He raced after it, barking and snapping as it bounced in crazy directions over the uneven grass. As he lay munching his apple, I held my hand out.

"Mom gonna get it!" I teased, and his play snarl-bark said: *No you're not!*

"No, Mom not take your apple!" I laughed, as I remembered Sammi's old prune-blop game.

Archie was such a teaser. Holding the apple in his mouth he'd eye me, his thumping tail asking for a replay, while Spanky would get in on it, too, looking up at me slyly, growling and wagging as he guarded his big apple treasure. But they both enjoyed the game more than eating the apples, so Rosko had easy extras.

Dusk came earlier each day and fall chores began. I bid my garden beds goodnight for the winter, pulling the last few errant weeds and raking away the remaining leaves. Our firewood delivery signaled the cold weather was imminent, and as we loaded the woodshed the pupz "helped," making off with the smaller logs, hamming it up for the delivery men, and jumping inside the trailer to search for mice under the wood. The rest of the winter-prep chores followed: disconnect and drain the hoses, wrap the barn hydrant in heat tape and insulation, and get the horse blankets ready. A winter's worth of hay, delivered and stacked, made the barn cozy, and it smelled so wonderful! MüFarm was settled, the pack was healthy and happy, and all were ready for winter.

But in early 2016, tragedy struck. On January 14th, while driving to her riding-therapy volunteer job, our dear friend Susie was killed in an automobile accident. It was a crushing loss. Mike and Susie were part of our family, and we did our best to support Mike while dealing with our own grief. Susie had been part of our lives since our first day on MüFarm, and between us many animals had come and gone. Through the good and the bad, we were always there for each other. Never again would her car pull in the driveway for an impromptu visit, or to drop off a pan of her fabulous homemade granola power-bars. It seemed impossible she was gone.

Susie's memorial service reflected her life, overflowing with family and friends, tears, laughter, prayer, and memories. A large table filled with photographs showed Susie with her children, riding her horses, or walking with her dogs. It was a healing experience but the devastation remained.

The days went by in a blur, but my most vivid memory is her Golden Retriever, Ellie, sitting on the front porch watching the long, sloping driveway, waiting for her mom. Once again, the blanket of sadness dropped heavily down over MüFarm.

Spring brought a bit of fun for Kevin and Rosko when they took a quick trip to Grand Haven, Michigan. For several years, Kevin had entered his paintings in a big arts fair in Grand Rapids, and one year he made a stop in Grand Haven to see how it had changed since his Coast Guard cadet days in the early 1970s. From an industrial shipping port to a bustling tourist town, Grand Haven had been transformed and he fell in love with the place, developing relationships with several galleries and businesses that displayed and sold his watercolors.

This time would just be a quick art-delivery trip, with a one-night tent camp at Grand Haven State Park, right next to the beach. Rosko loved going places, and was especially happy when it was only Dad and Rosko. Dad let him get away with stuff Mom would frown upon, and schedule-wise they winged it.

After arriving late in the afternoon, a quick swim was in order, and then Kevin picked up a calzone to go from a local restaurant. Leaving it on the dashboard, he ran into the gallery, delivered the art, and came back to discover half his dinner was gone.

"At least you left me half!" Kevin laughed at Rosko's guilty look. *Well, it's three hours past my food time, Dad, what did you expect?!*

After setting up the tent, they ate, went for another swim, and sat watching the sunset over the lake. Then it was Dad and Rosko in their little tent, crammed in between the monster RVs, with Kevin covered by 100 pounds of Rosko. Two happy boys off on their own adventure.

Archie had earned the rank of Allowed Outside Unsupervised and each morning included Perimeter Patrol: a ramble with Rosko down into the hayfield, sniffing and hunting and slowly circling back to the house. Just as Müsta had watched over Sammi, Rosko now took care of Archie, their black and blonde tails waving together above the hay.

Archie was nearly two and still full of puppy energy, but as much as he looked like Sammi his personality was different. He played ball but didn't fetch, preferring to catch a ball thrown high over his head or as it bounced from the ground. He didn't invent games himself but he loved it when we came up with something new, so we got very creative. Standing under the lollipop maple, Kevin would throw the tennis ball up into the branches and leaves while Archie waited, head cocked, and tried to catch it before it hit the ground. But after several tosses, he'd lose interest and we had to find another activity.

To vary the field hike routine, we sometimes took the pack west along the road, leash-walking the mowed berm. Unfortunately, there was a fair amount of litter and we never knew what they'd find, which made it more fun for Archie. Choice pieces he carried all the way home: an intact pizza box (sans pizza), a McDonald's bag, or sometimes a stick or tree limb so big it dragged behind. Neighbors and passersby got a kick out of him trotting down the road with his prize, and his antics became local legend.

But Archie was exactly like Sammi when it came to grooming; Archie hated being brushed and expressed his opinions through many different barks and play growls. In my experience, the amount of grooming a pup needs is directly proportionate to their dislike of the process. Grooming Sammi had been a challenge; Archie *really* made me work. His Husky coat picked up everything and his undercoat was very thick. Several times each spring and summer, I'd coax him out to the backyard for a grooming session, but as soon as the brush came out his ears would droop and his pace slow as he skulked toward me: *Oh, no, Mom's got the evil brush!*

"Archie, do your bonk for Mom."

That was all it took, and down he'd go. But rather than simply lie down, he'd melt into the ground, flop onto his side, put his front paws up in self-defense, and the growl-fest would begin. As I'd done with Sammi, I made a game of it—I allowed Archie his play snarls as long as he laid still. He'd start with strong objections, snarling and raising his upper lip a little to remind me he was *not* happy, all the while thumping his tail to show he wasn't really serious.

Brushing the thick scruff around his neck relaxed him, then he'd doze as I worked my way down his back and through the thick hair on his hips, before rolling him over to start again. His fluff-tail was last, earning me one more growl: *Hey, that's personal property back there!* Then he'd make his getaway, and the sparrows would swoop in.

Ranger — 2017

Evidently, the stray-dog network passed the word that Mü-Farm was the place to hang out. We certainly took in our share over the years. Returning home after dark one evening in mid-summer 2017, my headlights swept across the yard, startling a dog lurking near the barn. What a friendly, handsome boy! Mostly cattle dog, his pointed ears stuck up above intelligent brown eyes, and his short, sleek coat was black, with a gray mottled chest and black and tan legs. Hoping he'd stay around so I could find his owner, I gave him some dinner and closed him in the barn for the night. The next morning after breakfast our pack came out to meet him; they were curious but accepted yet one more stray. We called him Ranger.

Sarina lived nearby, so on her way to the shelter she stopped with her scanner, but he wasn't chipped. Since the shelter was full we were happy to keep him for a while. Like our long-ago stray visitor, Odie, Ranger loved hanging around the barn and yard, playing with our pack or sleeping in the shade; unfortunately, he wasn't a groundhog hunter. The days went by and no one called looking for him, which was strange—he was a very nice boy and was fine around Ramsey, so he must have been someone's farm dog.

When a kennel opened up at the shelter, Sarina came to pick him up, and as we sat outside our barn, talking, Ranger lay between our feet.

"C'mon, Ranger, let's go," Sarina beckoned, as she opened her truck door. Ranger put his paw in my lap and our eyes met.

"You're welcome, Ranger," I said. "You'll find a happy new home soon."

My promise came true. A few weeks later, Sarina and her husband adopted him themselves. Their good-sized property and small herd of cattle meant Ranger would have a farm of his own and a wonderful home. It was ideal for everyone, although it turned out he was afraid of the cattle, preferring camping trips and lounging in the house after a long day of supervising the farm work. Such a tough life!

Aside from our adventure with Ranger, summer 2017 was marked by our final major house project, the completion of the kitchen—probably the first item on most home renovation lists. I dislike cooking and spend as little time as possible in the kitchen, so I didn't really care how it looked. But the rest of the house was complete so it was time to finish it off. We replaced the old flooring, built a separate laundry room area, painted the cabinets, and installed a new countertop. Keeping the old-farmhouse feel, the 1950s Tappan stove remained and we added an old high-back porcelain sink.

By now, the pupz were used to us tearing stuff up so their supervision wasn't as intense. But they hung around anyway, helping the contractors. When it was time to paint, the four hairballs were banished from the area, but even with plastic taped over the doorways and all the guys outside, there will forever be hair from Rosko, Boo, Spanky, and Archie embedded in the kitchen paint on MüFarm.

Chores, remodeling, and critters didn't leave us much spare time—or money—for vacations, and planning one was always a trick. But after Kevin raved about Grand Haven, we'd taken a long-weekend trip in fall 2016. I, too, was hooked, and fall 2017, saw our first real vacation in many years. Since BooBear hated the water and loved Auntie Monica, Cousin Gracie, and the kids, he camped out at their house while we took the rest of the pack for a week-long getaway.

Grand Haven was such a dog town! Everyone seemed to have a dog or love dogs, and wherever we went our three were always a hit. Many shops put water bowls outside to welcome critters, while dog walkers and joggers stopped to share information on the best parks for hiking, and restaurants with pet-friendly outdoor seating. It was the perfect vacation spot and before we even settled in, our 2018 trip was already in the works.

Our Airbnb accommodation was close to the heart of the walkable downtown and a short drive to the ultimate destination—the beach. By mid-September, tourist season was over and the sand and beautiful, clear water were nearly empty. It was pup heaven! The water stayed shallow out across the sandbar so Rosko charged in, barking with joy, crashing through the waves with Kevin and riding them in toward shore. Swimming was Rosko's all-time favorite activity and the Lake Michigan water was his elixir; he'd turned 11 the previous March but at the beach he became a puppy again. Soaking wet, his patented Flop 'n' Roll in the warm sand turned his shiny black coat—from head to tail—into a giant sugar donut.

Intimidated by the waves, Spanky and Archie enjoyed swimming in the shallows and walking with us far down the beach, picking up bits of driftwood. Back home, at Alum Creek, Spanky's favorite game was Skippin' Stones, where he'd swim madly after small rocks we'd skip across the water. Undeterred when they sank, he'd just circle back, barking for more. Grand Haven Beach had no stones, so we'd skip a little piece of driftwood close to shore and he'd wade in, watching as it receded and rode in on the waves until he could grab it. Proudly carrying his Skippin' Wood to the beach he'd then roll on it, grinding the sand into his coat, before barking for another round. As he would with Skippin' Stones, he played as long as we threw the wood, rarely letting us relax.

Energy-boy Archie loved the wide-open space, running with us up the sand and across to the dunes, rolling in the scratchy dune grass. Hunting for dead fish was another favorite activity and, like Bear, Archie's cast-iron stomach allowed him to eat just about anything without upset (unless we counted his odiferous emissions). With his thick undercoat, he kept cool with frequent dips in the lake, then he dug a sand hole and curled up in the shade between our beach chairs, content to be near us while his brothers played.

Meanwhile, BooBear was getting completely spoiled by Monica and the kids. Unsure of where he was at first, he hid in an upstairs closet, but soon realized his begging skills went a long way in the kitchen. Since old Gracie slept most of the time, Boo was the center of attention, snuggling on the couch to watch TV with the girls or hanging out with Monica as she cooked. Non-stop attention and treats were Boo's idea of a vacation!

Exploring the Grand Haven area, we discovered new swimming spots and hiking trails along the coastline, packing in as much activity as possible; between the sun, waves, and sand, the week disappeared. But as much as the pupz loved adventures in new places, there was nothing like the scent and familiar routine of home. We all missed Boo and MüFarm.

CHAPTER 16
Old Pupz: 2018

bobo

Another old dog with nowhere to belong, his eyes showed a mixture of hope and resignation. We couldn't resist.

Social media is my blessing and curse, keeping me in touch with all my dog-loving friends but also tempting me, multiple times each day, with pleading eyes and forlorn faces. Sharing the dogs' photos with my connections widened the network to help find them homes—just not mine, please! But in early 2018, there was BoBo and my "sucker for old dogs" button was pushed again. It's not like we actually *needed* five pupz, but this one reminded us of old Poppa. We knew that Rosko and Boo would be fine (they got along with everybody), but we took Archie and Spanky with us when we drove to the Holmes County Shelter.

BoBo was certainly old. The mist of cataracts clouded his eyes and his muzzle and eyebrows were graying. Showing some stiffness in his hind end he moved slowly, but wagged his tail and tried to trot toward us as we knelt to welcome him into our hearts. He was smaller and more compact than Poppa, his head was narrower, and while his coat lacked the black points, its color, texture, and undercoat were the same—oh, boy, another shedder!

Outside, he wandered around and sniffed, never standing still, and the warden said even in his kennel he paced and barked, making it clear he didn't want to be confined. Archie and Spanky sniffed and wagged briefly, then set off to explore the shelter's play yard while BoBo followed along. It was obvious they considered him no threat, so home he came to MüFarm.

Yahoo! A new brother! BoBo passed the Rosko and Boo-Bear sniff test too, and Rosko immediately did the play-bow, hoping for some rowdiness, but Bo showed no interest. Happy to be out of the noisy, bewildering shelter, he ate dinner, tagged along on the evening walk, then crashed on one of the pup beds, quietly content through the night.

Until they learned the scent of home, our new rescues were always clipped to a tie-out line when we weren't outside with them. Big mistake with BoBo! It was immediately apparent he'd never been on a line before, and he kept getting totally wrapped up and tripping himself. But it was also obvious he was right at home on MüFarm, following us around or lying down nearby. He was easygoing, undemanding—except at food time—and, like Poppa, was happy to watch the goings-on around him.

Not much into the plush toys as playthings, he enjoyed using them for pillows; he'd pummel one of the dog beds into submission, then plop down with his big head squarely on a toy. From Goodwill, we'd collected several large, floor-pillow-sized stuffed animals, all now in various stages of wear and tear: the tips of Red Crab's gray legs were chewed off, Green Bunny was missing half an ear, and I'd mended the giant yellow Tweety Bird so many times it eventually had to be thrown out. With the exception of KatKat, the guys shared all the toys and beds, understanding it was first come, first served, and Bo happily took whatever bed and pillow were left.

On Bo's first Shammi Sunday, we headed for Mount Gilead State Park rather than overwhelming him with the dog park. Leash-challenged now with five, Archie and Spanky went on ahead with Kevin while I walked the two slowpokes; Rosko free-ranged between us. Bo was a perfect match for Boo's ambling pace, two sniffers who checked out every tree and log, pausing to decide if the spot was pee-worthy before moving along. I enjoyed the slower pace, too, taking in the quiet of the woods, and as I watched the conga line sniffing and marking, it struck me: somehow, of all our pupz, Lapsi had been the only female. While we'd chosen Müsta, the rest were the luck of the draw, and the male-dog marking competition was just part of life.

With all five pupz, their toys, and their beds crammed in together, my home office was now very cozy. The futon was prime real estate and vying for a spot was a daily challenge. If Rosko got there first, there wasn't much room for anyone else except Spanky; if Archie was first he'd stretch out, rolling on his back with feet sticking out, claiming the entire futon for himself. With two or three beds in front of the futon it was really one giant bed, and I'd step carefully over the big sleeping pile—with wall-to-wall dog beds, who needed carpeting?

Bo learned my workday schedule, joining the noon field walk and poking along with Rosko and Boo. Rosko was 12 years old and arthritis slowed him a bit, but he wandered along, rolling in the hay now and then, thrashing in ecstasy and leaving a big, mashed-down spot behind. Along with his arthritis we were also watching a small, slow-growing, benign bone tumor above his right eye. It didn't bother him and was growing out away from the eye socket, so we left it alone, telling him it gave him extra character—as if he needed more.

Personality-wise, BoBo reminded us of Bear, with the same sweet innocence clear in his eyes; his simple, happy outlook; and his love of food. Feeding time was still a raucous event, and we discovered on day one that we needed to feed Bo separately; Rosko and Archie didn't appreciate Bo barging in front. Not a fan of being shut in the Rosko Room, Bo demanded, *Hurry it up!* with his huge, deep bark. As we'd come down the steps toward the gate, he'd start his chow-time happy dance, bouncing up and down, hopping from one front paw to the other, unable to contain himself. It cracked us up every time!

He amused us in other ways, too. Although Bear had never been a graceful pup, he was at least semi-nimble—BoBo was a total klutz. When feeling frisky, he'd try to join in the pack play but his clumsy old body would have none of it. So he'd bounce around, barking at the goings-on until his energy gave out then he'd plop down. And as his cataracts thickened he tended to lose track of himself, bumping into things or getting himself stuck.

That summer, while having some work done on the barn, a contractor came daily for about two weeks and parked his 4x4 pickup in the driveway. The other pupz got used to him, and after hitting him up for treats they'd go off to find other things to get into. But BoBo barked and carried on as if each time was the first time. One morning, the big Bo bark continued and Kevin followed the sound—there was Bo, stuck under the truck, which was just high enough to clear his back. Evidently, Bo hadn't seen the truck and kept walking, hooking his collar on something and requiring Kevin to crawl in after him. But overall he was an easy boy, happy in his retirement and content with his place on MüFarm.

In late August 2018, we added one more grave to our Memory Garden when Mouse, our old house cat, passed away. In 2000, not long after Red had joined us, she'd arrived on Müfarm as a tiny kitten; her long life spanned 10 pup-pack generations. As we dug her grave Rosko, Boo, and Bo didn't pay much attention, but Archie and Spanky sat close by, very aware their little play pal was gone. As he'd done with Shaman, Spanky whined softly, gently pawing her face.

Grand Haven 2019 would be 10 days of fun and sun, and Monica stepped in to take both Boo and BoBo. Boo looked forward to being spoiled again, and how much trouble could old Bo make?

"You'll need to feed him separately, so maybe out on your front porch," I suggested. "But don't put him on a tie-out line since he's clueless and gets tangled up. He can't move very fast and won't go far, anyway."

Famous last words. After arriving in Grand Haven, I received a frantic call from Monica early Monday morning.

"Bo is missing!" she cried into the phone. "I fed him outside and when I went to get him, he was gone. It was only a few minutes!"

Since she got up very early for work in Columbus, it was still dark outside, and since Bo was quite deaf, calling for him did no good. After checking MüFarm several times she drove around the nearby roads, but he was nowhere. She was frantic with fear.

Calming her the best I could, I posted a profile and picture on our local missing-dogs Facebook page—I'm not sure why, but I had a feeling it would all turn out OK. Among our many dog-loving friends, anyone who saw the post would be on the lookout, and we got lucky. A friend replied right away about a found-dog post that looked like Bo, so I scrolled down and there he was, safe at a kind woman's house. She'd found him walking along the roadside, and he'd climbed right into her car. I called Monica and she sobbed with relief.

So much for not moving very fast and not going far! Somehow, he'd managed to get about two miles away, on the road, in the rural dark without getting hit, which was a miracle. Thanks to our Facebook network, and a kind-hearted neighbor, he made it back safely, although Monica gained a few gray hairs.

After Bo's great adventure, our week in Grand Haven was wonderful. We were even closer to the center of town this time, there were no stairs to challenge Rosko, and off the back of the house were a deck and small fenced area for relaxing after a day of beach activity. We rebooked it for 2020 immediately. Nearby was a little town-square-style park with a fountain, oak trees, and many acorns and squirrels; Spanky was on constant watch as we looped around "squirrel park" on our morning walks. Rosko was noticeably more limited this year than last—he could do the park, but we now drove them all downtown for our stroll along the Grand River channel. Sidewalk leash walking was not a skill our farm pupz had mastered, but they did their best. High tourist season was over, the crowds were gone, and leisurely evenings of outdoor dining found the guys sitting or lying by our chairs, alert for dropped crumbs.

Hikes this year were shorter and took longer as we kept an eye on Rosko's energy level, playing the bad guys when it was time to turn around. According to him, he was still a youngster and wanted to go for miles, keeping up with Archie and Spanky and even breaking into a run occasionally. But hiking out also meant hiking back, so we chose our trails to match his endurance, pacing all of us so we didn't wear out before the long week was over.

Most days we spent at the beach, and I entertained Spanky and Archie while Rosko followed Kevin for a swim, ending up on the sandbar out near the buoys to watch the boats go by. On windy days we stayed at water's edge, washed by the sun and breakers, then sat back, hypnotized, as kite flyers and kite surfers filled the sand, waves, and sky—rainbows shooting across the water, rippling against the bright blue.

Back at home, we unloaded everything and headed over to pick up Boo and our wayward BoBo. Monica felt so guilty, that somehow the whole Bo episode was her fault, but *I* was the one who'd told her to feed him outside without a tie-out. It could have turned out badly, but the pack was safely back together and we were grateful to Monica and her family, and to the neighbor who rescued old Bo. He'd certainly taught us a lesson.

Although I could hardly bear the thought of leaving Mü-Farm, my gardens, the Memory Garden, and everything the place meant to me, Grand Haven began stirring in my head as an ideal place to live. I'd sold Ramsey in 2018; my arthritis wouldn't let me ride anymore and I'd found an ideal buyer, so I said goodbye to my horse-owning life and now the barn stood empty. Retirement was also on my mind, but two monumental changes were too much to contemplate together, so moving remained in the background for the time being. The pupz had guided most of my major decisions so far—I'd just wait for their input on this, as well.

One drawback of rural living was the distance from things city-dwellers take for granted: shopping, friends, and a variety of restaurants and entertainment venues. But as COVID-19 took over everything in 2020, being remote and relatively isolated became a huge advantage. My home office meant work wasn't affected, but I watched, virtually, as my office-bound colleagues around the world also became tele-workers, and for some the transition was difficult. Masking was commonplace whenever we left MüFarm, and my regular Saturday shopping trips to town became less frequent as retail stores and service providers carefully felt their way through the COVID guidelines. Many closed face-to-face interactions, providing remote services as best they could.

Vet visits were our biggest concern since Maple Run wasn't allowing owners into the office or exam rooms, even wearing a mask. While completely understandable, it made getting care less convenient. But we all did what was necessary. Fortunately, there were no emergencies, and for scheduled visits the staff would shuttle the pupz between our car and the office. Archie and Rosko thought it was a blast—they could misbehave the whole time with no Dad or Mom to scold them, and both took shameless advantage. Bo and Boo didn't mind the arrangement, either, since the techs always gave them treats. Spanky was the only one who worried. He was all happy and wiggly to see the tech come out, but then: *Oh, no, Mom's not coming!* His ears would droop, he'd turn back toward the car, and the tech would carry him inside.

Somehow, the COVID rampage missed Kevin and me, but watching the nightly news and seeing the chaos in the hospitals made us realize how bad it was and how fortunate we were to be out in the sticks.

A long-standing dream of ours was to have a fence around MüFarm, but the expense had always held us back. For 25 years we'd been vigilant about the pupz not getting in the road, but as southern Morrow County became more developed, the vehicle volume on our little road increased. It was no longer the sleepy back road we knew and loved, and Bo's recent escapade made us realize we couldn't tempt fate any longer. Through a contractor friend, we hired an Amish crew who did beautiful, affordable wood fencing, made dog-safe with woven wire. At 7:30 a.m. on May 12, 2020, the crew showed up with a huge trailer loaded with fencing material and a walk-behind fence-post pounder, and by 5:00 p.m. the project was complete. It was the first-ever MüFarm activity the pupz couldn't help with. The new fence completely enclosed the yard, connecting to the pasture fence from the northwest corner and running all the way around and down across Turner Trail to the southeast corner. The pupz now had secure access to the three-plus acres of yard and pasture, and finally even BooBear could be free.

Without his tie-out line, Boo walked around his familiar area and then kept going, following the fence line, checking out every interesting smell and critter hole. It was nearly dusk when, far down in the pasture, he stopped and looked up in surprise, as if he were in alien territory. Over the next few days, his newfound freedom began to show in his personality. Whereas before he used to wait until we took him out, he now went to the door and barked, demanding we open up, then he'd stay outside for hours, roaming the enclosure and discovering all the groundhog holes. His stiff shoulders wouldn't let him move fast enough to chase them, but he spent many hours nose to hole, barking and digging, happier and more content than we'd ever seen him. Damn the expense—we should have put the fence in years ago.

Kevin and I were happier, as well. Out in the yard we no longer worried at the sound of an approaching car, scanning quickly to be sure the guys were close by. If a critter or stray was across the road, the pupz would bark and charge the fence, but we didn't have to chase frantically after them. It was a huge load lifted, and neither of us realized the weight of the worry until it was gone.

Only Archie was put out with us. He was used to his daily Perimeter Patrol down Turner Trail and around the hayfield, sometimes with Rosko but usually on his own. It was his solitary time, Mr. Independent Archie, and now he had to wait for a field walk with the pack. Frequently, to give him a thrill, we'd let him out the Turner Trail gate so he could go check on his property. When Rosko went along, the two of them would wander the field for an hour or so and then bark outside the gate, our security guards reporting back. It was a good compromise.

As 2020 progressed, it became clear Rosko's time with us was drawing to a close. He'd turned 14 in March—amazing for a Lab—and his age was catching up with him. For the past year we'd cared for his rectal polyps, watching them come and go and then come back again, and we treated the accompanying off-and-on diarrhea. At his age, there was nothing we could do except have Dr. Mooney monitor them and keep him on medication. She stressed that we needed to clean him carefully, so each time he came in from the yard, into the tub he went for a gentle wash; not his idea of fun, but he accepted it as he did with everything. The bone tumor above his eye was now the size of a ping-pong ball but it didn't bother him, and the eye below it was still normal. Somehow, both his eyes were clear of cataracts. He remained our happy Rosko, a little gray around the muzzle and paws but still full of himself, keeping up with the normal activities as best he could. We looked forward to our fall Grand Haven getaway, with the growing knowledge it would probably be Rosko's last.

Boo and BoBo continued to hold their own. Boo was right behind Rosko in age, turning 13 in July, and other than arthritis and mild cataracts he was still healthy, although a little hard of hearing. Bo couldn't do stairs anymore, so the ramp came in handy once again, and he was taking a supplement for sundowning—evening anxiety—which caused him to pace and whine until he tired himself out.

Both of them would have to stay behind again for our trip, but being displaced to Monica's would have increased Bo's stress level, so this time they needed to stay on Mü-Farm. Bill and Susie (another Susie in my life!), our good friends two houses away, would be moving to Idaho shortly after our Grand Haven trip, and Susie offered to come and stay with them. They both loved dogs but didn't have one of their own, and Susie especially loved BooBear. Spending time with them would be her last dose of pup overload, and the fence guaranteed no escapees.

Preparing for the trip, we planned for Rosko's needs and his changing system, packing up the doggy diapers and pads left over from Poppa's last days; Rosko hadn't needed them yet, but we brought them, just in case. Several years before, Kevin had widened the treads on a three-step, foldable ladder, making it easier for Boo to get in and out of the car, so we brought it along for Rosko.

After the long drive, we unloaded and headed to the beach. Barking and chasing, Spanky and Archie raced each other to the water with Rosko not far behind, his old legs moving with happy purpose. By the time we caught up, they were already soaked and sand-covered. The setting sun colored the horizon as we walked down the beach, watching as the Lake Michigan magic turned back Rosko's clock, his age and infirmities vanishing in the waves. Grand Haven was his special place.

But the travel upset Rosko's system, and we were up and down with him throughout the first night, wondering if the trip was a mistake. In the morning, a local vet agreed to see him on short notice. Due to COVID, we couldn't go in with him, and as we relayed Rosko's history to the vet tech, he hammed it up, showing off his Rosko Flop and then happily following her inside.

The vet came out and reviewed how serious Rosko's condition appeared, gave us some medication to try, and broached the topic of euthanasia as "an understandable option." Not according to Rosko—not yet! The medication evened out his system, and the rest of the week he was nearly normal. He was such a rock.

Our hearts told us this was his last hurrah, so each day was a treasure of stored memories and pictures. With age, he'd became more vocal, barking for attention as if he knew his time was short. Inside the house we kept him quiet, but on the beach he could make as much noise as he wanted—off-season, there were few beachgoers to annoy. His limitations guided the activities and one of us stayed with him while the other walked the shoreline with Spanky and Archie.

One afternoon, as I walked back up the beach, I saw them together, Kevin sitting next to Rosko as he lay in the gentle waves at water's edge. Dad and his boy, so happy. From far away I heard Rosko's bark and the sound, mixed with the waves, was as if from a dream, a precursor of time to come.

Early mornings found Kevin and me on the deck enjoying coffee, with the pack at our feet, while each evening we sat sipping wine and savoring the day. In between were walks and swims at any one of several beaches, watching the pupz enjoy everything. Outdoor restaurants weren't an option this visit, so we either got takeout or cooked at the house, dining on the deck with the pack. The daily activities tired them all out, especially Rosko, and he'd lie flat in the fading sunshine, snoring and happy. His formerly squishy body was losing the fight against time and his weight was beginning to drop, but his eyes and tail still showed the happy boy inside, telling us all we needed to know.

The week went by way too fast and packing up to head home was bittersweet. Our Airbnb hosts were fond of all our pupz but said a special goodbye to Rosko, and he responded to the extra attention with his usual silly antics. *He* didn't know there was anything special about this trip or this goodbye; now was good enough for him and he was happy.

Home again, we took the days as they came with Rosko's ups and downs. Kevin and I continued the routine of caring for Rosko, cleaning him up multiple times a day, giving him his medications, and keeping a close eye on his behavior. Time was short for him—his legs were weak and his system was failing, but his eyes still said: *Here I am!*

As Bill and Susie's moving date approached, Eric and Monica helped us plan a surprise farewell party at MüFarm one Sunday evening. The day was busy with house cleaning and food prep, and as we scurried around, it seemed as if Rosko was not quite himself. Normally, he loved party activities, "helping out" by being right underfoot, but he napped quietly all afternoon.

That evening, after the surprise was sprung and we were all enjoying the party, Rosko laid in The Café by himself. I went to check on him and Monica was there, sitting on the floor and petting him, his bufflehead in her lap. Our eyes met and agreed that he was starting to move away.

When the end is imminent the choice is usually theirs. Sometimes it's ours. Sometimes it's brutal and abrupt, and we have no option but to accept it. Throughout our years of loving pupz we've always done the very best we could for each of them. We'd watched Rosko so carefully, adjusting his diet as needed, giving him the prescribed medications, keeping him clean and applying fly spray. But somehow, even our best, all our care and vigilance, was not enough. It will be on my heart forever. It was not enough.

Monday morning, October 12th, started normally: all the pupz ate breakfast and were enjoying the morning yard. From my office window, I saw Rosko lying near the driveway in the shade cast by the cars, and he looked uncomfortable. Kevin and I went out to bring him in and clean him up, but it was so nice and sunny I brought the shampoo, sponge, and bucket of warm water out to the back patio. Rosko was tired and laid down, so I knelt and started washing him, gently working the shampoo under his tail and into his coat.

Suddenly, I saw a maggot! Without warning, like a scene from a B-grade horror movie, maggots boiled from the skin at the base of his tail, dozens of them streaming out as I screamed and cried, shocked, ashamed, and so terribly sorry. As they fell squirming to the concrete, Kevin and I stomped them with a fury.

Rosko lay still amid the chaos, his eyes calm and far away. It must have been such a relief, and all I could do was cry. We'd let our boy down; we failed him. Kevin took over rinsing him off and I called the vet; they said to bring him right in—we all knew what it meant. I texted my boss "dog emergency," then we carried Rosko to the car. This was *not* what we wanted for him, to leave MüFarm forever in a frenzy of noise and tears. But a peaceful end under the lollipop maple, surrounded by his pack, was not to be.

The vet staff met us at the back door with the gurney and wheeled him inside. I was in shock, numb with grief and shame. Dr. Mooney examined him gently, but aside from administering a drug to kill any remaining maggots, given his age, his polyps, and the condition of his system, there was nothing more we could do.

Disbelief and despair washed over me; the failure was overpowering. I was suddenly a child again, struggling with my studies, watching as the tape dispenser flew across the room, crashed against the wall, and landed—cracked and broken—on the floor. All the lessons and successes of my life vanished. Had I learned nothing in all those years?

We wrapped Rosko in our arms. I looked into his eyes with all the love in my heart and saw, looking back, what had always been there—deep love, trust, and calm acceptance—then we said goodbye to our Rosko.

I will never get over it, never forgive myself.

They don't judge, they never accuse. They only love and then leave us to deal with the aftermath. Over the next days and weeks, I struggled mightily to bring some sense to what happened. We were so careful! Only neglected dogs, ones no one loved or cared about, suffered such a fate. It couldn't happen to one of ours. But it did. I could not come to terms with it—I'd failed Rosko, and he paid the price. I couldn't apologize or make it better, there was no way to atone; the weight would always be on my heart.

The truth stayed hidden, and it was nearly two years before I told anyone else. I could barely admit to myself what had happened and certainly couldn't tell others. On vet visits with Boo, Spanky, Archie, and Bo I had trouble facing Dr. Mooney, and while Kevin and I shared the responsibility, I blamed only myself.

To everyone else, we simply said Rosko fell apart. With his health issues and advanced age, his passing was not unexpected and they gave us their sympathy and support. But that only made it harder.

For a long time, MüFarm was forlorn. We leaned on the remaining pack to get us through, but they shared our heartbreak and knew their Rosko-brother was gone. Since he'd been cremated, there was no last sniff, no graveside gathering, and without the chance to say a proper goodbye there was no touchpoint, no place in time for the loss. Spanky was the most aware, always on the lookout for Rosko's return. We were, too.

Two months before he died, I shot a video of him on one of our field walks, coming slowly toward me down through the hayfield at his old-dog, wiggle-butt pace. If I could reach through into that world, feel his soft squishiness, his black velvet coat all warm from the sun, I'd bury my tears in the whole of him and beg for forgiveness. In his eyes would be only love. I watch for him, always, to be following behind me. If I turn quickly and wait long enough, I'll see him. I miss him so much!

One consolation we held onto was his last trip to Grand Haven. Even with his serious health issues, he'd fully enjoyed the sand and swimming. At Hoffmaster Beach, he'd lain at water's edge, staring out across the waves, with his gray muzzle and eyebrows, and his bone growth, clearly visible. But on his face had been pure contentment. The memories are a golden halo in my heart.

CHAPTER 17
Monumental Change: 2020

müfarm

"Home is not a place, it's a feeling that you carry with you wherever you go." — *Author Unknown*

Sometime during late fall 2020, I discovered that my thoughts about Grand Haven had been rattling around in Kevin's head, as well, and we began talking about moving. Rosko had been with us for so long, and MüFarm didn't seem right without him. We were still in shock over the loss and—for me, at least—contemplating moving helped redirect my thoughts. Retirement was now heavy on my mind and we decided that if we were going to make a move, we should do it and get settled while I was still working. There was never any question where we'd go. We loved our Grand Haven getaways, so why not go and live on vacation?

I set Zillow and Realtor.com alerts for the Grand Haven area and in the spring, we started getting MüFarm ready to sell. The big projects were done, but 27 years of accumulated "why did we ever keep this?" stuff was everywhere, and we got busy. Our Grand Haven Airbnb was already reserved for the end of September, so we set a goal of listing the house toward the end of summer 2021.

Between work, getting the house organized, and taking care of the pack, I was dealing with both the nightmare of Rosko's loss and the idea of actually selling MüFarm, driving away for the last time and leaving it with someone else. Could I really do it? Practically, it was the right thing; it was too much to care for now and too big for our needs. But we'd poured so much of ourselves into the house and gardens—especially my beloved hosta beds—it gave me shivers to imagine the property in the hands of someone who didn't love it as I did.

And all those graves! The ashes of Shaman and Rosko would move with us, but eight dogs, two horses, and several

MONUMENTAL CHANGE: 2020

cats were buried on MüFarm, not to mention those whose spirits inhabited our Memory Garden. We'd planted six trees there for lost family and friends.

In the evening golden hour, I'd sit on the glider in the three-season room with the pack at my feet, savoring everything around me. Overhead, the wind chimes moved in the gentle breeze, the sound as much a part of MüFarm as the mantle clocks. My heart wasn't sure I could leave it all behind.

I also agonized over Laverne, our remaining barn cat. Shirley, her MüFarm mouse-patrol partner, had passed on in 2017, and while Laverne was still healthy, she was very old and quite frail. She'd been an outdoor cat all her life and moving her indoors in Grand Haven would be upsetting for her. Even though she was old, I couldn't euthanize her just because we were moving, and I would never leave her behind. With several months to go before our move, I decided to take a "wait and see" approach.

Spring came, and BoBo began having more trouble. Drops from an eye specialist helped with his cataracts and eye irritation, but his hips were getting worse so we blocked all the stairs. He spent his days either in the studio with Kevin or sleeping in the living room. At night, his sundowning anxiety now required calming medication so we could all sleep. While his appetite was still good (like Bear and Boo, Bo never missed a meal) he could no longer manage his food-time happy dance and we raised his bowl up to make eating easier. Bo's quality of life was declining but his eyes said he was still with us, so we stayed the course.

By early summer, we resorted to the old-dog belly-band and pad at bedtime and moved him into the Rosko Room each night. By day, he soldiered on, but the anxiety medication was no longer calming him through the night; a stronger one helped him sleep, but made him so sluggish in the morning he couldn't get up. We switched back to the previous meds, but by then he was turning inward, and on the morning of July 12th, he was ready for his journey.

The evening of the 11th, he was unsettled, barking and whining, unable to sleep, so I spent the night with him in the Rosko Room with his head on my lap. By morning we were both exhausted. Even with help, he didn't make it outside in time and he showed no interest in his breakfast. After notifying my boss, I sat with Bo a while longer in the sunny backyard, and once Kevin was ready, the pack gathered around to say their final goodbye. Then we carried Bo to the car.

During the drive he was very anxious, whining and struggling to stand, so I crawled in back and sat with him, petting his head to calm him. As he relaxed, his time with us came back to me, and I remembered his first Thanksgiving. I'd bought a fresh turkey and rinsed it, balancing it in the sink to drain. When I returned to the kitchen, there was Bo, looking up longingly, doing his little happy dance and trying to reach the countertop: *Mom, something up there smells really good!* If it hadn't been for the arthritis in his hind legs, that turkey would have been history. A smile wedged its way through my tears.

Moving him from the car to the gurney, and then into the clinic, was difficult, and after checking him over, the vet confirmed what Bo had already told us. As the sedative took hold, we held him close and he finally relaxed into the big sleep—not even a year after Rosko's death, another of our pack was leaving us.

Goodbye, big, sweet, klutzy Bo. Memories of your happy dance, and the sparkle in your eyes at food time, will be with us always.

Cremains from Shaman, Rosko, and now, BoBo, would join us on our move to Grand Haven.

After 11 years, there were again only three tails waving above the MüFarm hay. On our field walks, Archie and Spanky would charge ahead while Boo tagged along, taking two short, choppy steps with his front legs for every one he took behind. He was the senior now, healthy except for his shoulder arthritis, and as he poked along I frequently looked behind me, expecting to see Rosko and Bo bringing up the rear. No matter how many times we'd faced the loss, while each one was unique, the void was the same.

Field hikes were our respite amid the purging, downsizing process and the pupz kept us balanced as the moving plans progressed. The real estate market was getting crazy, and our listing date of the third weekend in August was fast approaching. Coordinating selling our house and finding a new place in Grand Haven was going to be a trick; it was a good six-hour drive between the two, so we needed a fall-back plan. Working with our Airbnb host we juggled dates, arranging to arrive earlier than planned and stay through the end of October, if needed. It was ideal since the house was big enough for all of us, and it would give us time for house hunting. Plus, except for Boo, our guys had been there before so their stress would be minimal.

Suddenly, it was time to begin saying goodbye. Our families were excited but very surprised—after all we'd put into MüFarm, most had been sure it would always be our home. Our neighbors Eric and Monica were devastated. Their kids grew up during our friendship, and between us we saw many animals come and go, sharing the joy and pain. With the loss of Susie Baird, and later Bill and Susie's move to Idaho, our circle of friends had dwindled and we'd grown even closer to Eric and Monica, relying on one another for advice, critter-sits, and deep friendship. I felt guilty leaving them, but no matter the miles, we'd always be neighbors.

Dr. Mooney was our vet and our friend, and it was hard to say goodbye. She and her staff had cared for our critters for so many years, with us through the best and worst. Our history with her made the thought of finding a new vet for our guys very unsettling—even more unsettling than finding new doctors for ourselves.

Saying farewell to Sarina, Crystal, and Kim at the dog shelter was also painful. Knowing how much they loved each dog under their care, and how much they relied on their volunteers, it was difficult to take away even our small contribution. Over the MüFarm years, we'd adopted six from the shelter, and our support for the staff would always be unwavering.

Two weeks before our For Sale sign went up, I let the church deacon know, then delivered a short note to each of the neighbors' mailboxes. As the news spread, neighbors stopped by to hear about our upcoming adventure, to say goodbye and wish us well, and the reality of our decision began to hit me. Our rural corner was close-knit, and I'd miss the familiar faces and the comfort of being part of such a wonderful community.

Even though I was excited about the move, sometimes during the chaos of organizing and packing I'd stop, stand still, look around, and remember. All the MüFarm critters would come back to me, their favorite sleeping spots, the sound of their nails against the hardwood floor, and the echoes of their barks, meows, and whinnies. Sammi's spirit still walked the upstairs rooms and the others gathered around, as well. Müsta and Lapsi were with us at the beginning of MüFarm—how long ago that seemed—and I realized we could mark the years by which pupz we had when, and what house projects were completed.

In 1997, Sammi and Bear occupied the renovated second story with us. In 2002, Sammi, Bear, and Red saw the completion of the three-season room and porch—a Sammi paw-print remains forever embedded in the front-walkway concrete. Shaman missed the 2015 addition of the Rosko Room and The Café by eight months, and Rosko only enjoyed the 2020 fence for four months before he left us. Their lives paralleled ours, passing the time with such joy and making everything worthwhile. They would always be part of the house.

I also remembered all the love, money, and hard work we poured into the place, tearing out plaster and lath, hand-sanding the uneven wide-plank oak and maple floor boards, painting, fixing, and maintaining. It figured that just when all the remodeling was finished, we were moving! But the house had a life of its own, a personality and character. It had sheltered and protected many families and generations since it was built so long ago—it was time to say goodbye and let it care for new owners. Hopefully, they would also love and appreciate it.

Packing the house room by room took *so* much time—everything I touched had memories attached so I was easily sidetracked, especially when packing the pupz' stuff. Among our current pack, none were very interested in balls or stuffed toys (except KatKat) but the old toy bucket still sat in the living room, and as I dumped it into a moving box, the pupz came tumbling back. There was Bear's favorite soccer ball, Shaman's Green Fish, and Rosko's Buzzy Bee. Then, an old Brain Ball rolled out, hitting the floor and emitting its familiar squeak, a sound I hadn't heard in many years. Shaman and Rosko were fetchers but they'd preferred tennis balls. Müddha was our last Brain Ball maniac and when he died the era ended; as one of his last toys, this one belonged on MüFarm. I placed it on his grave, next to his headstone.

In addition to packing the house, the barn and other outbuildings also needed sorting out. Even though I'd sold Ramsey, I hadn't really been ready to admit my riding days were over, and so my horse-related items sat in the barn: water buckets, feed tubs, blankets, lead-lines and halters, and the big tack-trunk full of all kinds of useful things. Keeping my treasured saddle, I donated everything else to a local horse-rescue operation to use as needed and put the rest in their annual barn-sale fundraiser. After loading everything else into their truck, we used the dolly to roll the heavy trunk up a ramp to the tailgate. From Missy's days as a show horse to her last days, the trunk, with its perpetually squeaky hinges, had been a part of daily barn life. Watching it all drive away brought tears.

MONUMENTAL CHANGE: 2020

In the end, I gave my saddle to Ally and Viv, Eric and Monica's daughters—a saddle is meant to be used and I'd never ride again. The last link to my life with horses, it was hard to give away. But it went to the right place.

As it turned out, our move was timed perfectly. The real estate market was red hot by the middle of August, but even so, I held doubts about the house actually selling very fast—maybe deep inside I hoped it wouldn't sell. Cleaned and purged, after the real estate team finished staging the place, it was so beautiful we didn't want to leave! But Kevin was excited about living in Grand Haven, which made it a little easier for me. MüFarm was too much for us now—too much land and too big a house—so I kept my focus forward.

The listing went live on a Thursday morning with a Sunday night deadline for offers, so Thursday and Friday found me working from Monica's while Kevin took the pupz and vacated MüFarm. We spent evenings at Alum Creek since the showings were booked until 8:00 p.m. each day, and Saturday and Sunday were equally crazy with non-stop showings. By Sunday night we were ready to have our house back.

All the showings meant forthcoming offers, but when our Realtor, Becky, and her partner, Nina, came on Monday to review everything, we were dumbfounded—41 showings had resulted in 11 offers!

Along with the offer we accepted was a buyers' note from Andrew and Ashley describing how smitten they were with our farm and its history, and how they wanted their two young children to grow up on the property. But two other comments in the note told us they were the ones: Ashley's grandfather was a deacon at the Baptist church across the road and Ashley had attended services there as a child, *and* they owned a cut-flower business, which they would expand over the MüFarm acres.

As I read the letter out loud, even Becky and Nina were in tears. The church congregation was family and Ashley's connection completed the circle. But for me, knowing my plants and gardens would be loved, cared for, and expanded gave me such peace of mind. All the worry and tension of the previous months were suddenly released; we could now let MüFarm pass along, knowing it would be in good hands.

Boo, Spanky, and Archie immediately sensed our relief and we celebrated with a Penlan Park hike. There were next steps to take soon but we needed some special time to relax and have fun; the previous four days had been turned upside-down and we all wanted our normal routine. The second-cutting hay was finished and the large round bales sat scattered around the field, so each evening we took walks through the hay stubble, letting the pupz ramble and sniff as long as they wanted to, since our MüFarm days were now numbered.

As the moving date drew closer we continued working on cleaning out the sheds and corn crib. We sold several items to our buyers for their flower farm, and gave them other tools we no longer needed. There was still a lot to get rid of, but somehow it got done and the outbuildings were nearly as empty as the day we moved in.

One evening, walking to the house from the barn, my eyes swept the backyard and I spotted Big Red, forgotten next to the pup pool near Sammi's grave. My eyes welled up. I could hear Sammi's high-pitched bark as he pushed it across the yard, and I saw Müddha carrying it to me, drop-

MONUMENTAL CHANGE: 2020

ping it and demanding Big Red Bowling. No one had played with it since Müddha died 13 years ago but there it sat, waiting for some other pup to come along. I left it where it was.

Of all the things we were leaving behind, I worried most about the pupz' sense of place, especially BooBear's. Mü-Farm had been his home for so long, his safe and secure place; Grand Haven would be a big change for him. But one thing we'd learned is how adaptable pupz are—wherever we went they were happy, as long as they could come, too. I still worried about Laverne, but as we'd cleaned out the barn and outbuildings, she watched, unfazed, from her favorite spot under the old lilac. Hopefully, she'd adapt as well.

Our stay at the Airbnb began on September 16 and our contract with Andrew and Ashley gave us until the end of September, if needed, so there was plenty of time to organize the final details before getting to Grand Haven and looking for our new home. But the week after we accepted the offer on MüFarm, my Zillow alert found an interesting house, so we made a quick weekend run, leaving the pack with Monica overnight. We toured three houses on Saturday afternoon, and by the time we returned home on Sunday, we had an accepted offer on a little ranch in Spring Lake, right across the river from Grand Haven. The yard was made for the pupz, although we needed to put in a fence (again!); the drive over the bridge to Grand Haven Beach was about 15 minutes, and hiking paths and state parks were everywhere. Once again, the pupz' needs were the driving force.

Wednesday, September 15, 2021; the end of an era. Our real estate contract closed and MüFarm officially passed from our care. Over the previous weeks, Andrew and Ashley had become good friends, sharing with us the plans for their flower business, Bel House Farms. Walking the property, we discussed sun exposure, water access, and all the other stuff gardeners love. Talking as we walked, I pointed out each pup and kitty grave, where Missy and Gunner rested, and the meaning behind each Memory Garden tree. The magnolia we'd planted in memory of my sister had flourished, enveloping the plaque bolted to the boulder beneath, and spreading slowly down the slope, self-rooting as it went.

"I hope someday the kids will be married in this garden," Ashley said. "And I promise to care for Sue's magnolia." Her comments went to my heart, knowing she and her family would add their own memories to our special place. Andrew and Ashley were also animal lovers, having rescued and adopted dogs in the past, including some older ones; we shared the stories of our adopted seniors.

A meet-the-neighbors party that evening introduced them to everyone and they fit right in with the group, instantly at home, just as we'd been on our first MüFarm day. Their two children played with the neighbors' kids back near the pup pool, and soon Big Red was again bowling across the yard, chased this time by a pack of happy, boisterous kids. The gathering also gave us one more chance to say farewell—we'd do final packing the next day, then head to Grand Haven. Closing on our new house was set for Friday morning, which happened to be my birthday.

Our last day on MüFarm wasn't exactly as I'd envisioned it. Such a large undertaking guaranteed several snafus and way more last-minute things to be done. The movers were late and packing the truck took longer than expected; we were running out of time. One car was dedicated to the pupz, Laverne's crate, and all their stuff, and we couldn't fit everything we wanted to take with us in the other car, so we left some items in the three-season room to pick up on a return trip. By the time the truck left and we were fully loaded up it was nearly 6:00 p.m., and we had a long drive ahead. I'd wanted to take a quiet walk through the empty house, one last field hike with the pack, a silent moment in the Memory Garden, and a stroll around the yard—saying goodbye to the graves, my gardens, and my hostas. But there was no time.

Kevin drove out the gate first, so closing it for the last time fell to me. Standing outside, I looked back at the house—the windows, the porch jump-off spots, barn, and pup pool now so empty. I imagined myself standing in the living room, the mantle clocks and wind chimes packed away, and the silent house pulled at my heart. But I knew it was waiting.

My hosta beds were nearly ready to go into the ground, and the remaining leaves moved in the gentle breeze, waving goodbye. As the gate-latch clicked, the tears started, and continued off and on, until we were nearly halfway to Grand Haven. Leaving was incredibly hard for me.

Spanky felt my upset even though I tried my best not to show it, but the stress of the last few weeks, and my sadness, could not be contained. He fretted over my tears for a while, then settled down with his KatKat and the three pupz slept quietly, unaware they'd just left the only home they'd ever known, and the sights, sounds, and smells that were part of their souls. I again thought about the graves left behind—pupz, horses, and cats—and all the joy, loss, and lessons of the last 27 years. I tried to look forward, knowing this was the right move for us, but my head could not yet convince my heart.

Goodbye, MüFarm. We remain forever a part of you, and you a part of us.

Exhausted both physically and emotionally, we finally arrived at the Airbnb well past midnight. After unloading everything, we set up an enclosure for Laverne—she was very upset but finally settled down—then everyone fell instantly asleep. After closing on our new house early the next morning, Kevin got back in the car for an overnight round-trip to MüFarm to collect what we'd left behind.

Then, I went to check on Laverne. She'd been quiet in the morning and I assumed she was sleeping, but when I opened the pen I knew immediately something was very wrong. She was breathing but unresponsive. Frantic, I called the vet that had seen Rosko in 2020, but they were booked. Finally, I found one willing to take an emergency; I wrapped Laverne in a towel and rushed to the clinic.

There was nothing to be done. In the exam room, I removed the towel and Laverne stirred, tried to stand, but wobbled, then fell. The doctor said she'd probably had a stroke. Due to her age and frailty, I decided to let her go; I held her gently as the vet gave her peace.

I'm sorry, old girl. I never should have brought you with us. You should have passed away on MüFarm, to rest forever under your lilac tree. I did what I thought was best, but I was wrong.

I had Laverne cremated and the following spring, I took her ashes back home to Ohio, to her shady spot under the lilac.

Between Kevin's drive to MüFarm and back, and Laverne's sad ending, we were all in need of some Sunday evening beach time to rest and regroup. Monday, my workdays would resume and new-house projects would begin, but for now we walked the shoreline, taking in the Lake Michigan tranquility and watching the pupz have fun.

The Airbnb remained home until the end of October as contractors worked through fencing, flooring, and painting at the new place. As we unpacked the basics and got the new, temporary routine established at the Airbnb, Boo completely surprised us; he was unfazed by the move and all the upheaval, following us around for a while and then curling up in his bed. Evenings and weekends were spent at the new house, setting up the kitchen, moving furniture into place as projects were completed, and walking the pupz around their new neighborhood. Everything was exciting, for all of us.

In mid-October, we headed back to Ohio, to retrieve the last of our stuff from a storage locker in Mount Vernon. The drive took us through Mount Gilead and as we drove the familiar road toward the entrance to Mount Gilead State Park, the pupz all sat up: *Oh, boy, it's hike time!* Their ears drooped as we passed the park. When we approached County Road 20, the turn-off road to MüFarm, they barked with joy—*We're going home!*—and I was surprised by my flood of emotion.

In Mount Vernon, we picked up a U-Haul truck, loaded up our stuff, then spent the night crammed together in a friend's small apartment before heading out early the next morning.

This time, driving away felt final; my sense of home had shifted. Two weeks later, we moved out of the Airbnb and into our house; our pack and all our stuff were finally in one place again—we were officially Michiganders.

Of the three pupz, the move affected Archie the most; the fence wasn't complete yet so it was back to the tie-out lines. Boo had gotten used to his freedom on MüFarm but didn't complain too much, and Spanky was such a people boy he didn't want to be outside unless we were with him, anyway. But Archie was totally insulted! He tolerated the line but was *not* happy about it, and he laid in the backyard with a scowl on his face.

"Just a little longer, buddy," I promised. He wasn't buying it.

He missed his long rambles through the MüFarm fields and the freedom to do as he pleased, so we made it up to him with extra exercise. A short walk from the house we discovered the Minnie Skwarek Nature Preserve, our new Penlan Park, with trails looping through the trees and a creek winding back and forth under narrow wooden footbridges. The hike was too far for old Boo, but Archie and Spanky were happy, noses to the ground, sniffing the wildlife scents that crisscrossed the trails and disappeared into the woods.

As the days passed, their sense of place grew and it didn't take them long to recognize their new home, and the scent of NüFarm. After Boo became comfortable in the new house, we left him home with a special treat so we could take Archie and Spanky for a run on the beach. Even in winter it was beautiful, and with no one around the pupz released their pent-up energy, racing over the sand. Ice mountains built up along the shore as the waves slammed in, spraying up and over like geysers, and nature reclaimed the ungroomed beach. The wind came in unimpeded across the water, blowing over and around the snow fence, depositing gritty sand/snow dunes in the parking lots and roadways. It was hard to imagine that in a few months the tourists would be back, basking in the summer sun.

NüFarm lacked a fireplace, which I missed, but the house stayed snug and warm as the snow piled up outside. Boo spent the days in his favorite bed, wrapped in his old spider blanket, now time-worn with a few small holes. As we unpacked boxes, Red Crab and Green Bunny emerged and when Buzzy Bee appeared, memories of Rosko bounded back. Too many trips through the wash had silenced the bee's little song long ago, but the joy it had brought him was unforgettable. I placed Buzzy Bee atop Rosko's urn.

From the last box of pup stuff, I unwrapped the two very heavy Roseville ceramic bowls, beige, with DOG in brown letters. It's funny how certain things are so much a part of life that you barely even think about them. But as I lifted the bowls from the box and set them in their new spot, my mind's eye flashed on Müsta, splashing his little puppy paws, practicing his swimming. The sound of happy lapping came back to me across the years, with memories of the tidal waves of slopped water we'd mopped up. Thirty-seven years and 14 pupz ago, we'd bought the bowls for our firstborn, and they became one more link across the pack generations.

Everyone received a belated Christmas present in January 2022 when the fence was finally completed. The back part of the yard and beyond the fence was wooded, the critter smells were everywhere, and the squirrel population was over the top—sometimes the race to the fence was very close. Boo hopped around in the snow, bundled in his quilted jacket, happy to wander where he pleased until his *Let me in!* bark demanded his warm bed and blanket. He amazed us every day, carrying on in the face of his increasing mobility challenges. When he walked, his elbows twisted out awkwardly and his front feet crossed over each other slightly, now taking three of his choppy front steps for each hind one. His cataracts continued to thicken and his hearing was fading, but he never missed the sound of food dropping into his bowl. In many ways, he reminded us of Bear; he never complained or fretted, was always happy, and never asked for much, except at mealtime.

Winter in Michigan was Archie bliss! His Husky undercoat grew in thick and warm, and he spent most of each day out in the snow, sleeping in the sun on the back deck or under the front roof overhang. Nestled in the snow, oblivious to the cold, he'd snooze away as flakes accumulated on his coat.

"Archie, want to come in?" I'd ask through the door crack.

He'd open one eye: *You talking to me?* Clearly, he was content.

If it's going to be cold we want snow, and January and February didn't disappoint. What we didn't count on was the ice, and even the longtime locals were surprised at the thick layers covering the sidewalks. Snow removal is serious business in Michigan and the crews are good at it, but even cleared, the walking paths were treacherous. For more than six weeks, the weather remained in a deep freeze. The sun-melted snow would refreeze each night, thickening the ice. Boot cleats allowed us to walk safely, but we were very careful of the pupz, especially BooBear; a slip and fall, broken bone, or dislocated shoulder could mean the end. He never went outside alone and we steadied him up and down the three steps to the yard. We all missed the MüFarm ramp.

Actually, I was the one who had trouble with the ice. The deep snow of a mid-February evening drew me to nearby Central Park, and with my cleats forgotten in the car, Archie, Spanky, and I avoided the ice-covered paths, walking slowly in the drifts and enjoying the crisp winter quiet. The little township park bordered a huge old cemetery, beautiful with its white-capped headstones washed in moonlight and the remaining wind-tilted Christmas wreaths half-buried in the snow. Chilled and ready for home, we were almost back to the car when ice hidden under the snow took me down. I fell hard and heard a snap; my left wrist was broken.

Spanky hurried over, licking my face: *Mom, you OK?* Shaking with mild shock, I managed to get up, get the pupz in the car, and drive home, working both the steering wheel and stick shift with my right hand. After a trip to the ER and a temporary cast, I got the once-over as the pupz sniffed the strange-looking, odd-smelling thing on my arm—it was my first-ever broken bone. Throughout my childhood and all my horse-owning years, somehow I'd managed to stay in one piece.

The real adventure began the next morning, as I started to figure out how left-handed-me was going to manage for the next eight weeks. Kevin did most everything at first, as I gradually trained my right hand and took over a few chores. But eating remained awkward and I dropped food like a child, making me very "pupular."

After I got my permanent cast I could go outside (with cleats on), but none of my winter coat sleeves fit over the cast, so I dressed in funky-looking layers and made a mitten out of a wrapped scarf. Everything was jerry-rigged, but we figured it out and I was continually thankful I hadn't broken my hip. Also, if I was going to break something, I was glad it happened in the winter. A cast on the beach would not be much fun.

I'm the first to admit I make a terrible patient. Like my dad, I'm fiercely independent and can't stand not doing things for myself; the daily challenges got old fast. Cooking and doing dishes fell completely to Kevin; about all I could do in the kitchen was make coffee and feed the pupz. Fortunately, Kevin enjoys cooking—if it weren't for him I'd have starved long ago—and has never balked at doing dishes, but I was frustrated I couldn't help. My woe-is-me self-pity party ended after one especially trying day when, remembering the patience and determination of Lapsi, Red, and Müddha, I found the inspiration I needed: adapt and work around challenges. I reminded myself that my situation was temporary, which made things easier.

March 15th, my retirement date, crept closer. Each day was spent on a screen-share call, training my replacement, trying to cram my 30-plus years of experience into six weeks. Running my keyboard one-handed slowed me down considerably, but we got through it. Retirement was exciting to contemplate; I'd been looking forward to it for a long time, but as it drew closer, I was sad. (Well, only a little.) It would be strange not interacting daily with my team, those friends and animal lovers who'd been part of my world for the past 12 years. The Friday before my last day, the team threw a virtual retirement party and it was nice to be with them all one last time, even though it couldn't be in person. Each shared a memory of our time working together, and the one from Todd, my boss, brought me a few tears.

"Nancy's best advice: When you're stressed, take the dogs for a walk; it fixes everything." It *is* good advice, but all credit goes to my life with pupz. They taught me that a long time ago.

Then the day was upon me and I couldn't call Todd to say goodbye without crying. More than my boss, he was a friend and animal lover extraordinaire, supporting me through so many joys and sorrows, including the passing of Shaman, Rosko, and BoBo. In the end, we messaged back and forth, said our farewells, and I logged off for the last time. The end of another era.

But I hadn't counted on how easy it would be to keep in touch with everyone—in the old days, moving away meant packing everything into boxes and leaving friends behind. Now, we folded everyone inside our laptops and carried them along. My long-established online connections brought me frequent updates; I easily kept up with Eric and Monica in the old neighborhood, Bill and Susie on their Idaho adventure, the ladies at the Morrow County Dog Shelter, and former colleagues and friends.

Zoom allowed Kevin and me to continue our attendance at the Mount Gilead Area Writer's Guild meetings, transporting us across the miles and keeping the creativity alive. As his artistic expression evolved, Kevin had transitioned his creative juices from painting to writing, and while I was sorry to see him take a hiatus from painting, the new medium inspired me, as well. I'd dabbled with writing in the past and now, without work and farm chores, time allowed for more literary endeavors. I wrote mostly nonfiction, based on personal experience, while Kevin's inner artist gave him the freedom to create short stories woven with a bit of fantasy and twisted by his sly, wry sense of humor. Our writing cohorts provided inspiration and encouragement, allowing us to follow our muses wherever they led.

Each time a monumental shift happened, the pupz always noticed it first. Accustomed to getting up with me each workday at 5:00 a.m., they were wide awake on the 16th even without the alarm going off. They slowly started allowing us to sleep until 6:00, but tummy-time is pretty inflexible. My wrist cast was still a bother; everything I did took longer and the pupz tried to be patient as I worked the can opener and handled their food bowls one at a time.

"Sorry, guys, a few more weeks." They cocked their heads, listening but not understanding. Pupz live in a right-now world.

Retirement confused Spanky the most. Always my little office helper, he'd slept under my desk or enjoyed lappie-time while I worked, and he didn't know what to make of this change. Now, after pup breakfast, Kevin, Archie, and Boo would doze off again for a while. Coffee on the couch became my special Spanky time, snuggling in the fleece as the clocks ticked in the quiet house and dawn crept across the snow. Gazing at me intently, he'd lift his left paw into my upturned palm and hold it there.

"Is that my paw? Mine forever and ever?" *Yes, Mom, forever.*

MONUMENTAL CHANGE: 2020

Work had always defined my days, too. I wasn't used to having time all to myself, and being housebound by the weather and limited by the cast made me stir-crazy. Like our long-ago Sammi, I'm a doer, always on the move and not one to have idle hands or an inactive mind. To save our sanity, Kevin bought me several jigsaw puzzles, set up a big table, and I passed many late-winter days slowly puzzling, one-handed.

Finally, in mid-April the cast came off and it felt so good to have my wrist and hand free again. During therapy, pup walks were still limited—I could walk little Spanky but not Archie—so for a few more weeks Kevin and I walked together as the snow melted, the days lengthened, and spring came closer. Able to wear my winter coat and gloves again, we started regular beach walks, watching the ice mountains melt along the shore and the city crews move the drifted sand back onto the beach with their Bobcats and bucket loaders.

Before Memorial Day, the official start of tourist season, Grand Haven held its Earth Day beach clean-up, a community event attracting an army of volunteers. Archie and Spanky enjoyed the exercise and attention as we walked the length of the beach and back several times, filling, emptying, and then refilling buckets—it was amazing how much stuff washed up in just a few months. Newbies to the sand-grooming process, we watched, fascinated, as the "beach Zamboni" provided the finishing touch, making passes up and down, whisking the sand clean.

By the end of May, with trash cleared away and rogue sand dunes subdued, the beach was ready. Bring on the crowds!

CHAPTER 18
Life on Vacation: 2022

spanky, archie, boobear

"There's no place like home. Except for the beach." — *Author Unknown*

Grand Haven had been our vacation spot for so many years that it surprised us now and then when we realized: we're locals! As the weather warmed, our little street came alive with dog walkers, joggers, and neighbors who stopped to greet us and meet the pack. Our fence enclosed about half the front yard, allowing the pupz to hang out on the porch and keep watch, barking as needed until everyone understood the yard belonged to them—for farm pupz, all the activity was very exciting. And they soon realized: *Oh, boy! The delivery people are here, too, and they have treats!*

Back in 2013, we'd jumped on the Chewy.com bandwagon, and it hadn't taken the pack long to recognize the delivery trucks as an opportunity to help out, and get treats. Rosko, especially, had hammed it up, jumping into the truck as the door rolled up and giving the driver his best belly-up flop with wildly thumping tail. Each pup then waited for a handout from the driver, their reward for a job well done.

Now, with neighbors close by, deliveries happened up and down our street daily, and even from inside the house the pupz knew the sound of an approaching FedEx or UPS truck. From the window they'd watch hopefully, not understanding why the trucks frequently passed them by.

During our first spring and summer on NüFarm we made the house our own, which for me, of course, meant gardening. Planning my new garden beds kept me busy, and the pupz tagged along as I unpacked the wind chimes and placed them around the yard. Before planting began, I cleaned out my tool bucket and decided that garden tools are like pup paraphernalia: I held onto stuff even though I hadn't used it in ages. Rooting through old weed diggers, spades, and mismatched gloves, buried under everything I found a small, dusty piece of cloth; it was a dirty, ragged shred of Red's old Green Gator. For at least 13 years it had hidden in the bucket, waiting for me to find it—how it got there, I'll never know.

Gardening is my Zen, my connection to the earth, giving me a sense of place and permanence. As I planted, the sound of the wind chimes drew me back to my MüFarm gardens, and I remembered Red, my ultimate garden helper. I found myself waiting for the feel of him leaning against me, and the touch of his nose on my ear: *Mom, it's break time.* Now, with Archie and Boo asleep nearby in the sun, Spanky sat next to me, supervising. I put my arm around him; his coat was all warm from the sun.

Between Memorial Day and Labor Day, dogs are banned from Grand Haven Beach between 11:00 a.m. and 5:00 p.m., so we explored other places, parks, and beaches, shouldering the backpacks and finding new adventures. On one trip to Hoffmaster State Park, we discovered the Walk-a-Mile trail, a beautiful up-and-down hike through heavy old woods full of wildlife smells. The trail ended atop a sand-dune cliff, overlooking a mostly deserted stretch of Lake Michigan beach. A slide-walk down the sand earned us all a cool-off swim.

It's inevitable that while on the beach, we remember Rosko. Our last vacation with him had included several trips to Hoffmaster and we know he's still with us, lying at water's edge. His joyful bark booms with the incoming waves and he rolls in the sand, feet kicking the air. It's so unfair he didn't get to live out his days on NüFarm, sharing with us the nonstop swimming and fun. In our hearts he's very much alive, and we find ourselves expecting to see him in the house and yard, sleeping in his new favorite spots, snuffling among the hostas and ferns, and hamming it up for the neighbors.

I still struggle with the loss, and although the ache is forever in my heart, time has given me perspective, a place to understand what he taught me. With his last look, Rosko gave me his simple gift, and my greatest lesson: from the peace and acceptance in his eyes came complete forgiveness. If, somehow, he was still with me, his love would be unwavering.

I understand now that all my life, while I'd learned from and accepted my mistakes, I'd still held them inside, beating myself up over my failures instead of forgiving myself and moving forward.

Rosko, I know I can never undo what happened, only accept it and somehow come to peace. This is a hard one. I've forgiven myself, but even so, I'm forever sorry, Sweet Boy.

Boo still does outings with us and after their dinner we take them to Grand Haven Beach, backing the car to the edge of the sand so Boo doesn't have far to walk. The early evening sun slants off the waves and the clouds glow pink and orange, blending with the colorful beach umbrellas scattered all around. Vacationers with tired children pack up and head for their cars as the dog people arrive. The workday is done and now it's pup playtime, fetching in the waves, digging holes, rolling in the sand, and breaking out with the zoomies—no matter the breed or mix, some dog behaviors are universal.

Even these short trips tire Boo out and he always sleeps extra soundly after beach time. Recently, he's become more vocal as his sight and hearing fade, and he comes looking if he loses track of us. All his life, thunderstorms never bothered him, but the booming vibration startles him now and among the three of them, an approaching storm means major upset, especially at night. Thundershirts help Spanky and Archie somewhat, but Boo's doesn't do much for him and he clings, shaking and trying to crawl underneath or behind me. Calming supplements don't help, so during overnight storms I resign myself to no sleep, sitting on the floor with three panting, trembling pupz plastered against me. I guess it's nice to be needed.

While our adventure here is still new, we often remark what a great move it was, and heading into our second fall, the pack is settled and content. Spanky is still my snuggle-boy, although he no longer jumps up on the bed or into the car by himself and sits waiting for his lift-up. He still runs and plays with Archie, and watching them in the yard or on the beach, it's easy to forget the passing time. Spanky is at least 10 now and in the sunlight I see silver mixing with the cream color of his face—my heart skips a beat.

With the chilly nights, the spider blanket has reappeared for another winter, wrapping Boo up in his bed, and each morning his wiggly-worm roll-around ends with him hopelessly twisted up in the blanket. Still our silly, happy Boo. Archie is in his glory, free in his yard, keeping the squirrels and bunnies on their toes or sleeping on the deck in the afternoon sun.

I love it here, too, but as the season turns I'm reminded of the winter-prep chores on MüFarm, the huge maples flaming red and gold, and endless walks through the harvested fields. I miss the quiet rural peace, the evening sun slanting through the trees, the old house standing watch over its corner; I'll always think of it as my home.

But my mom used to say, "Home is wherever you make it," and although I haven't moved a lot, I've lived enough places to know she was right. We've made our home on NüFarm and it's perfect for our place in time and for our pupz. As long as they're with us, we're home, no matter where we are.

Now, between adventures and taking care of the house and yard, surrounded by our pack of three, I sit writing the stories of their lives and of all those gone before. I find it easier to write about the ones who've crossed over. Their stories are complete and writing about them brings them back to me across all the years: the everlasting joy that filled our days, the losses that took chunks of our souls, and the learning they shared. I carry in my heart everything they taught me, and while I've known important people, dogs have been my greatest influence. Simple, non-judgmental, accepting of everything, forever loving, patient, and forgiving, they've lifted me up, moved me forward, and vanquished my failures.

As Boo, Archie, and Spanky snooze, their beds surrounding me in my office, I look at them and smile—simply having them nearby makes me happy. I know someday they'll leave us, as well, but for now I live in the moment with them, anticipating our next adventure.

As old Bear used to say: *Whatever's next, I'll love it!*

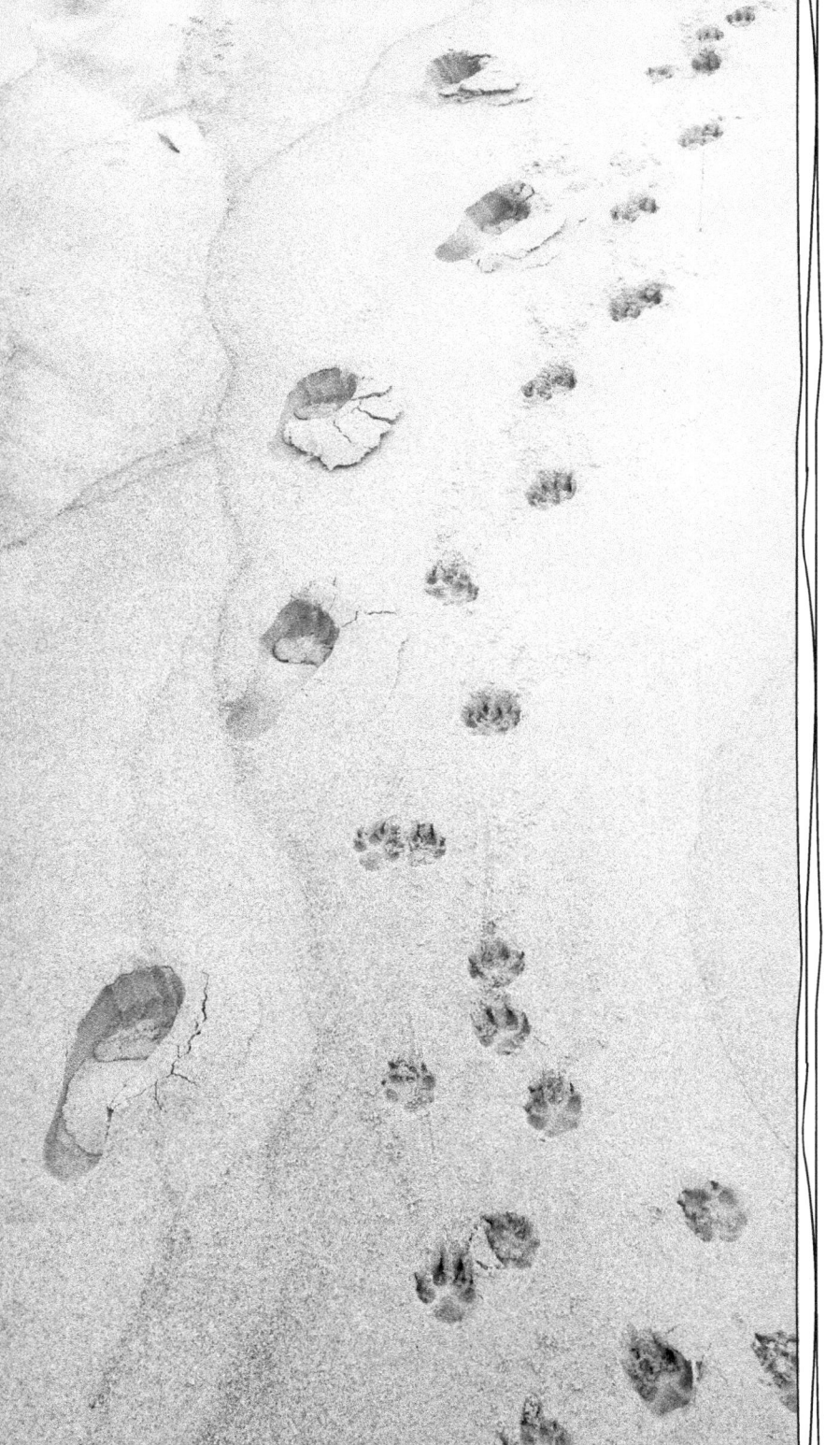

Epilogue

boobear

On April 15, 2024, at home on NüFarm, snugged in his spider blanket and surrounded by love, BooBear left our lives. Severe arthritis, fading kidneys, and a true but failing heart couldn't dim his will to try, and we helped him along until his struggle became too great.

No longer able to get up on his own, he could barely stand long enough to eat, and we walked him to and from the yard, then back to his bed, with a tummy-sling. As with Müddha, Boo outlasted his body, and his spirit hadn't given up when we had to make the decision. The five of us enjoyed one last sunny afternoon at the beach, sitting on the warm sand, gazing across the water.

For several days afterward, Archie seemed puzzled by Boo's empty bed and his spider blanket, washed and folded like a pillow, waiting. As if to fill the void, Archie and Spanky sometimes laid there, bringing us all comfort.

Boo had been an old pup for a long time. It's hard to remember him as a youngster, full of energy, hiking and hunting for hours, roughhousing with the pack, jumping on the bed with ease, and, of course, doing his wiggly-worm routine. Part of our lives for 14 years, he'd spanned six pack generations, from a humble, uncertain beginning to a secure and happy life. A chance was all he wanted. We gave him that, and in return BooBear gave us so much more.

Acknowledgements

My story results from a long and winding journey, which would not have been possible without, in equal measure, my husband Kevin and all the pupz of our lives. You've shaped and guided me, making me who I am today, giving me the support, love, humor, and confidence to put your stories, and mine, on paper.

To Cindy Collander, my late sister-in-law and forever friend. You lived this story with me but didn't get the chance to read it.

And to my family, thank you for your support and encouragement, and especially to my sister, Beth—your honest feedback on my first draft sent me back to the drawing board to begin again.

Eric and Becky, thank you, forever, for your design and creative talents, for bringing the images in this book to life, and for loving dogs as much as Kevin and I do.

To Kristin, my Editor-in-Chief, thank you for everything you did to make my story work.

To my beta readers, Ann and Linda, and especially Lora, who told me a memoir is not a memoir unless I put myself in it, including the "deeply personal stuff." Thank you, Lora.

Along my journey, encouragement, support, and inspiration also came from published writers including Lisa Rimmert, M.K. Martin, Deidre Fagan, Teresa Rhyne, Penny Neer, Scot Long, and the members of the Mount Gilead Area Writers Guild.

www.ingramcontent.com/pod-product-compliance
Lightning Source LLC
Chambersburg PA
CBHW020149090426
42734CB00008B/755